You
and
Your
Network

Getting the Most Out of Life

You
and
Your
Network

Fred Smith

WORD BOOKS
PUBLISHER
WACO, TEXAS

A DIVISION OF
WORD, INCORPORATED

YOU AND YOUR NETWORK

Library of Congress Cataloging in Publication Data

Smith, Fred, 1915–
  You and your network.

  1. Christian life—1960–   . I. Title.
 BV4501.2.S5324 1984   248.4   83–23578
 ISBN 0–8499–0373–4

With gratitude

To all those who have had part in the exciting life
I have been helped to live: my heroes, my models,
my mentors, my friends, my family—especially my family

and

To those who have chosen me as mentor letting me share
in their talent and success.

Bless these all!

CONTENTS

FOREWORD

In the course of a lifetime, one is indeed fortunate to encounter that unique other person whose impact is startling enough to be life-changing. That's the way it was with Fred Smith and me!

It wasn't exactly a meeting—more like an event. I was a college student at Baylor University; he was one of several business and professional leaders brought to the campus for Religious Emphasis Week. I had never before heard of a man named Fred Smith, and the name is really not that prepossessing. But since he was to address one of my regular classes during the week, I had no choice but to hear what he had to say.

Up to this point, I was honestly not very proud to be a Christian, except when I was with an inner core of dedicated Christians. Fred Smith changed all that for me. He was a forceful personality, a nationally known speaker, a high-level corporate vice president, an obviously intelligent human being—and still proud to stand before a college audience and talk about Christian commitment.

The closer I got to Fred Smith during this week on the campus, and on subsequent occasions, the more I came to realize his uniqueness as an individual and his genius as a thinker and observer of the human situation.

Fred loves to discuss—and to analyze people. Whatever the problem and topic for discussion, he always has the gift of seeing something which no one else is seeing. He can identify the essence of a problem more quickly than anyone I have ever known. And he can deal honestly with insights which most of us might care to avoid. If you don't want to have your facades and pretenses destroyed, you don't want to fool with Fred Smith. He would rather mess up somebody's imaginary playhouse than eat hush puppies, and he loves hush puppies.

Fred's early business career was with Genesco in personnel, and later in vice president roles with Powell Valve Company and Gruen Watch. He became quite well known as a labor expert and was a consultant to businesses with particular emphasis on labor relations. This grew further into general business consulting, which included such companies as Genesco and Mobil.

In the early years of Word, Incorporated, I asked Fred to devote some of his consulting time to our company. I appreciated the fact he was willing to do it, since he had choices of devoting his time and energy to some larger, more glamorous companies in the business world. His contributions to me personally and to Word through many years have been of signal importance. More importantly, his contribution to me as a friend has been beyond what anyone could measure.

I'm sure one of Fred's major callings in life is to expose phoniness wherever he finds it. This includes his close friends, the numerous audiences to whom he speaks, business executives with whom he consults and ministers and other Christian leaders whom he encounters in numerous ways. His incisive wit and biting insights won't let anyone he's around be overly comfortable. To those who are willing to be reasonably open around Fred Smith, there will be a lasting, affirmative contribution made to their lives. Unquestionably, he is threatening. Most of us don't like to be threatened and certainly most groups and institutions avoid it like the plague. That's all the more reason people like Fred Smith are needed. They can penetrate through our layers of self-deception and make us see the truth, even when it hurts.

Throughout his adult life, Fred has been one of the most effective public speakers in this country. He has been widely sought after for speeches to business and professional groups as well as to numerous church conferences, conventions, and retreats. His ability to read people privately, and in a public audience, is remarkable. Without question, he has been a tremendously effective speaker to public audiences with a true gift of sensing an audience's feelings and needs.

Fred has been a valued member of the Board of Directors at Word, Incorporated, for years. He is our "friendly flame-thrower"—even board meetings become exciting when he is present.

Over a period of several years, I have tried to persuade Fred to put some of his ideas and thoughts into print. While he has wanted to do this, I have also sensed his fear of doing so. Putting things in print is different from reading an audience and responding.

This book represents a major event in the life of Fred Smith. It's my hope that it will enable numbers of people to discover this unique person. Above all, I believe this encounter with Fred Smith will stir something within you, the reader, which will open new dimensions and higher possibilities for your own life.

JARRELL McCRACKEN

PREFACE

Living with a love of life is the best way to truly, deeply experience life. I wrote this book hoping that you might have "more"—more insight, more views, more expressions for the feelings you have, and more interest in the things you see and read. I wrote for those determined souls who demand more from life.

John Locke said it well: "We search after the truth as a sort of hawking and hunting wherein the very pursuit makes a great part of the pleasure." I aimed sincerely at truth and usefulness. And with two such good targets I may be excused that my bullet was of such small caliber that it made little imprint upon the target, but my shooting at least pointed to the target, at which you may fire your larger caliber gun.

I predict you will find two major faults: that I have said too little on some subjects and too much on others. I confess I meant to say all I had to say on any subject on one or two pages, but each subject grew out of my control. I will thank you greatly to winnow out the wheat and let the wind of your sweet charity blow away the chaff and whatever fluff I left upon you.

For your enjoyment I have put at the close of each section some one-liners which I hope you will read and reread in those small bits of time which make the difference in our lives. Those which I knowingly borrowed or suspect that I borrowed are in quotes; the others I believe originated somewhere in my own experience.

I

JOY FOR
THE JOURNEY

*Joy is adequacy for life. With it we become
survivors in a hectic world. Joy makes the journey
a profitable pleasure—a trip with meaning.*

enjoyed
this week

JOY FOR
THE JOURNEY

When I speak of "joy for the journey" I am not talking about surface happiness which comes and goes like the wind. Joy is more than happiness. It is the deep feeling of adequacy which the black preacher felt when he prayed, "nothing's gonna come my way that you and me can't handle, is there, Lord?" Joy is more than fortuitous circumstances. Who needs joy when everything is going right? We need it when life is out of joint.

Joy Is a Result

Oftentimes I have read of "secrets" of joy, but actually there are no secrets to be hunted and found like Easter eggs, or pried out of some mysterious guru, or found in effervescent books or discovered in esoteric cults. Joy is a result. It is a reward for life being well spent in hope. It is a result of the principles of maturity which the wise, the saintly, and the serving have all found and followed.

Joy is available to any normal, healthy personality. Perhaps there are certain neurotics (such as Dr. Samuel Johnson claimed to be when he said, "From my teens I have suffered a diseased spirit") in which melancholia replaces

17

joy. However, I'm convinced that if we've ever been capable of knowing joy, we can develop and control our emotions to the point where joy can find a comfortable, permanent home within us.

Recently a restive friend said, "I feel a lack of joy in my life. Sometimes I wonder if it is worth it." He seemed passive to life, acted upon by circumstances, pressured by events. He was absorbing the pessimism of the many who go about their daily lives, not realizing that joy is a result of what we think and do—most of which we can control if we have the courage to take charge of our lives.

Keep the Rainbow

A young preacher in his first pastorate in a small northern mill town was talking for his first time with the mill owner, who said, "Young man, you have not seen me in church and you will not see me until my funeral. I own this town and this mill. It is my pot of gold. When I came here, a young immigrant, I heard that in America there was a pot of gold at the end of the rainbow. I found the gold, but, young man, I lost the rainbow."

From the time God first showed it to Noah, the rainbow has been the symbol of hope—the promise of ultimate victory and of relatedness with the eternal and the divine. That hope and the joy it brings is what the mill owner lost. But he didn't have to. Life is rarely a choice between the rainbow and the gold. We can have both.

Once I spoke to a conference of corporate presidents in Canada. Following our meeting we were discussing personal success and how to define it. One of the presidents engraved his definition on my memory: "I would like to live rich as well as die rich." He had learned how to keep the rainbow and the pot of gold.

If you ever have to make a choice between living rich and dying rich, *choose living rich.* But I don't think many of us really have to make that choice. We can learn to have both by learning to choose our attitude toward life. But most of us fail to realize we actually do have a choice.

Choose Your Attitude

In his book, *Man's Search for Meaning*, Viktor Frankl sets forth this most significant idea: ["We have a right to choose our attitude."] Frankl was speaking from the desperate experience of a concentration camp where they stripped him of his family and even his clothes, making him dig with his bare hands in the frozen ground for food—a situation far more desperate than any of us have experienced. Yet he found that his captors could not take away his right to choose his attitude. And for this reason, he was freer than his guards, who absorbed their attitude from the inhuman Nazi regime. Because Viktor Frankl *chose his attitude*, he was able to work out his ingenious psychiatric theory of Logotherapy while in a concentration camp.

Shortly after reading Frankl's conclusion, "Ultimate freedom is man's right to choose his attitude," I was in New York on business for the week. Anxious to get a stand-by seat to Cincinnati, I failed and dejectedly went back into Manhattan to spend the night awaiting the 10:00 A.M. Saturday flight. When we got on the plane the pilots revved up the engines for a few minutes and then shut them down. Anxiously we listened to the captain's word on the intercom, which told us we had a four-hour mechanical delay. The passengers went into a tizzy, particularly one thin, tightly wound gentleman right in front of me who jumped up, grabbed his hat out of the rack and, with disparaging remarks about the canine ancestry of the airline's officials, bolted off the plane to tell the young woman at the counter (who, of course, controls all jet mechanical failures) what he thought of the way they ran the airline.

Irritated by the inconvenience, I decided this was a very appropriate thing to do, so I moved to join him. Nothing would be more effective than two fools up there screaming at some poor young woman who could do nothing but try to pacify two juvenile adults who had been delayed for four hours. As I stood up to follow, there came clearly to mind Frankl's definition, "Ultimate freedom is man's right to choose his attitude," and I sheepishly sat down, realizing I had not chosen my own attitude but had absorbed it from the circumstances and the people around me.

As I began to analyze the situation, I realized here were four hours of absolute quiet. There's nothing quite so quiet as a dead jet. I had a very comfortable seat and most attentive stewardesses to serve me free coffee, plus a briefcase full of work that needed doing. Those four hours probably were the most productive I spent that year. Actually, if I had seen an advertisement for a job with the same sort of favorable working conditions I was given on that airplane, I would have applied for it!

Ever so often, with a certain amount of embarrassment, I think of how I became an emotional slave for a few minutes and then, with Frankl's help, an emotionally free man. When we absorb our attitude we are slaves; when we choose it, we are free.

Give Yourself into Forgetfulness

The essence of joy is the willingness to *give oneself into forgetfulness.* We hear so much about "forget yourself," and that is a healthy admonition, but it's as difficult as trying not to think about a pink elephant for five minutes. We are so much with ourselves that we can't forget ourselves. However, by a determined, disciplined effort, we can give ourselves to some cause or person until we truly forget ourselves. John Wanamaker said, "The most important lesson I have learned is that I have the least trouble with myself when I'm giving myself to a worthwhile cause."

One evening I was sitting in the old Gibson Hotel in Cincinnati listening to two writers talking in the lobby. The younger one, in obvious admiration of the older, said,

"If you had your life to live over, what would you do with yourself?" Without hesitation, she answered, "I'd find something big enough to give myself to."

One of the truly nice stories I've heard concerned a young Amish girl who received a small box of candy for Christmas. Her mother, teaching her unselfishness, suggested she keep the candy unopened until her friends came by. After several weeks her friends came, and she excitedly passed the candy around, with each taking a piece. She closed the box and set it on the table without taking a piece for herself. When her mother asked her if she wanted some of the candy, she blushed and said, "Oh, I forgot that I was here." How many times the deep sense of joy comes as we give ourselves into forgetfulness.

Many people are literally sick of themselves. They become hypochondriacs *of the spirit,* thinking only of themselves without knowing that self-absorption is their disease. They are consumed with their thoughts about themselves and with what others are thinking about them—surfeited with self-image.

Unable to change their internal conversation with themselves, they go 'round and 'round, talking to themselves about themselves. Until this stops they have no opportunity for joy, and yet they want joy—but it won't come to those who are obsessed with themselves. It never has; it never will. The first essence of joy is giving oneself into forgetfulness.

I was once attending a laymen's meeting in a beautiful retreat. The group was reminiscing about the times when we were the happiest. A wealthy man, known for his grasping nature, relaxed enough to tell about an experience from his childhood. He had been saving money to buy a bicycle which he wanted very much when he heard a missionary tell of his work. The needs of this ministry impressed the young boy so much that he gave all of his bicycle money to the missionary. As he talked of this experience, the man was so overcome with emotion that he was unable to finish the story. I'm sure most of us wanted to whisper, "Do it again." Yet even knowing that this was probably the deepest emotion he had ever felt, he was not able to accept it as a principle—the door through which joy could once more walk into his life.

Make Others Feel Important

Another principle of joy is to *make other people feel important* and to do it sincerely. Once I was briefly visiting with a person of "seminal graciousness." As we talked, I noticed he was fingering a marble. Facetiously I asked if he expected to meet someone who might not have all his marbles to whom he might contribute. In some embarrassment he put the marble into his pocket and apologized for the distraction. When I asked to know what the marble meant, he handed it to me and around it was a gold band on which the Golden Rule was inscribed. He then explained how early in his life he'd had a great deal of difficulty getting along with people, until someone had suggested that he "make other people feel important." He used this marble to symbolize "importance," and whenever he talked to someone he lifted it in his fingers and symbolically gave it to them. It had become the foundation of his graciousness, for he truly had learned to make other people feel important and sincerely mean it by simply "giving them the marble."

From time to time we realize words in our vocabulary attach themselves to each other. For example, a person may be described as "proud and self-conscious." But joy is never attached to these two words. Even the most superficial thinker doesn't describe people as "proud, self-conscious, and joyful."

Feel Respect for Self

Joy comes to those who can truthfully yet humbly *know that they deserve respect.* We have an inner measure of what we feel deserves respect. Feeling respect for oneself is feeling that we belong in life. Alcoholics suffer from this loss of self-esteem. Unfortunately, some people never get the feeling of belonging. They feel forever out of place. Until they accept their right to a place in life, they never feel at home in life. Likewise, there are those who never seem to realize that they deserve respect and that it begins inside them. When anyone has done the respectable, they have become respectable. Former addicts of alcohol or drugs, for example, must consciously make a decision to respect themselves. Gandhi had this kind of respect, for he knew he personified a worthy cause in a costly way.

Bill Glass, who has been so effective working among prisoners, points out that low self-image is one of the common denominators of prisoners. He believes their low self-esteem led them into crime rather than crime destroying their self-image.

We deserve self-respect for many reasons. First, there is our potential to become a contributing, loving person. Then there is our self-restraint in preventing harm to others.

Furthermore, we deserve our self-respect by earning our way—by contributing more to life than we take from it. Mothers who may not have made an outside dollar in their life but who have raised their children well and held their families together have earned their way and deserve high respect. People in some of the lowest-paid professions contribute more than almost anyone. I particularly think of teachers.

Once I was talking to a retiring executive who said his lifetime ambition had been to "leave a better team on the field than the one I joined." And he did, by putting something into them that will keep on living after he is gone.

The wonderful thing about this concept is that if we weigh ourselves daily in the balance of life and come up short, we can do something about it immediately. On the other hand, joy is out for those who do nothing but accumulate guilt. And like self-pity, guilt is easy to accumulate.

Financial Integrity

There is also an economic requirement for joy—financial integrity. Those inundated by financial worries seldom exude a joyful attitude. Yet most financial problems are related to the one biggest psychological fault in most of us: our inability to delay gratification. We are so anxious for the fruit that we pick it before it is ripe. Oswald Chambers defined lust as "I must have it now"—and how true this is with most of us.

The *modus operandi* for our financial unhappiness is the installment system of buying which promotes the idea of having the benefits before you can afford the price. Our greed for things and our envy of those who have acquired them before us steals our joy.

There is some persistent quirk in our thinking that convinces us that temporal things will give us permanent joy. There is no doubt that new things will make us temporarily happy—but when we cannot afford them that happiness is soon replaced by anxiety and apprehension. Lust and joy are not bedfellows.

One of the most helpful disciplines ever given is Oswald Chambers' "Sit loose to things." Own them, enjoy them, expect them, welcome them when they come, but still "sit loose to" them. That way, if they go, they do not carry us with them. Things are to own and people are to love, rather than things to love and people to own. It isn't from the value of the car that we derive the value of the person who gets out of the car.

One of the most fortunate experiences of my life was being a poor but contented young man. And I do mean poor—I didn't have the seven cents carfare to ride to my date five miles away but I walked the ten miles without feeling bitter, envious or put upon. Being able as a poor person to be joyful has stayed with me throughout prosperity. I know from experience that material things (above the necessities) can neither bring nor take away inner joy. To be alive, healthy, and in a right relationship with God and man is available to most of us and this relationship brings joy with it.

Attitude of Gratitude

Another element of joy is the "attitude of gratitude." We have so much trouble believing "you have nothing but what you have received" thus we are totally, undeniably indebted to others. By gratitude we acknowledge our debt to others and through gratitude we relate positively. Hans Selye scientifically showed how, in his spectrum of energy use, gratitude conserved the vital energies of the person more than any other attitude tested. Those who live with this attitude of gratitude go through life with a great deal less friction and frustration. Their gratefulness lubricates their relationships and brings joy. Gratitude is one of our "push-pull" emotions. As we express gratitude, we feel it; and as we feel it, we express it—and so it grows with each push and pull.

Joy in Work

Work is essential to joy. Those who have learned to accept rather than escape meaningful work have added the element of joy to their labor. After Edison had worked sixteen hours a day, seven days a week, Mrs. Edison said to her husband, "You have worked long enough without a rest. You must go on a vacation. Decide which place you would rather be than anywhere else on earth and go there." Edison said, "Very well, I will go there tomorrow." The next morning he returned to his laboratory. He found joy, not escape, in work.

I contrast that with the story of one of my industrialist

friends who received a great deal of national, even international, attention for the hard way he drove his organization. One night in Denver he was seated next to me at a business banquet where I was to speak. Since he was getting on in years I asked him, "Have you thought of retiring?" "Yes," he said pointedly, "I've thought about it and decided against it because on my office desk are seventeen buttons, any one of which I can push and make something happen; . . . at home I haven't got a single one." Do I have to tell you that this was not a joyful man?

Joy and Health

Joy can live in a handicapped or sick body because it is a matter of the spirit. However, it can live more comfortably in a healthy body—one that is respected and kept from the abuse of excesses, including excessive adulation, pampering, or even excessive care.

Those of us who would have joy for the journey must protect our bodies from the diseases they can catch from an unhealthy mind. Whether we call them neuroses, psychosomatic illnesses, allergies, or by some other classification, they have their beginning as sickness in the mind and spirit rather than in the body.

I believe the AMA says that half the people in hospitals are there from a disease the body caught from the mind. Their diseases are real but they cannot be cured until the mind is cured. In a recent medical journal it was reported that general practitioners said that no more than 10 percent of the people who come to see them actually need to be seen by a doctor. When asked what they would like to do for the patient rather than give them some kind of placebo or tranquilizer, the doctors said, "Sit down and talk with them for an hour about their lives, their families, and their frustrations."

Often we must become our own doctor, our own psychiatrist or psychologist, and develop a mental control which keeps our minds healthy and prevents them from spreading disease throughout the body.

My family accuses me of an inordinate belief in the body's ability to cure itself. I can only speak personally, but I have found that when I have the right attitude my body has great recuperative power. This little slogan has been extremely helpful to me: ["There's nothing wrong with me that a little excitement won't cure."]

Very few people miss a vacation due to illness! Most of the school children who are sick at the stomach are sick of school. I have no scientific survey to prove this, but I would daresay that a class led by an exciting and loving teacher experiences less absenteeism.

Is hypochondria a communicable disease, particularly within the family? I think so. Fortunately, my family was not one that made a great deal out of sickness. My mother was a very determined woman whom sickness could not defeat. I have actually seen her place high-backed chairs around the kitchen and move from one to the other, holding on just in order to cook her family meals. For years I kept Kipling's poem "If" under the glass top of my desk, for the phrase "when nothing but your will says go" reminded me of my mother.

I am frightened that some families substitute sympathy for love and enjoy illness because it promotes sympathy—when love would bring out the discipline of fighting against the diseases of the mind that affect the body. I remind you that I'm talking about that whole body of diseases which are basically mentally incubated and foisted off on the body. These are the killjoys.

Furthermore, *joy is balanced by our sense of humor.* A sense of humor snuffs out our sparks of friction before they get to our fuel tank. We maintain a healthy humor muscle by exercising it. And that exercise program should include a massaging of our funnybone and a jogging of our ribs.

I am told that a sense of humor is severely lacking in practically all cases of insanity and psychological abnormalities. I believe it is also lacking in perfection, for it takes a sense of the real to see how unreal and funny we are. In one of our most fashionable neighborhoods, they are now saying that the mothers chuckle their babies by saying, "Gucci, Gucci, Gucci." That is funny because it is real but also unreal.

Of course joyful people expect the cycles—the ups and downs and the peaks and valleys of life—and not until they have experienced these, do they realize that their joy stays with them through all experiences of life.

Much of the chemical and narcotic problem in our culture is due to people trying to sustain themselves with synthetic joy. As they go into the valley, they try to fill it with alcohol, uppers, and downers, seeking to stay above the normal cycles of life. This is a disease and should be regarded as such.

Joy is not hypocrisy nor Pollyannaism. Joy is realistic. It knows that life is painted in light and dark colors—that it has its contrasts—but that growth can come in all these moods and times. Joy faces every situation with hope, faith, and a sure knowledge that there has been adequacy for the past and that the same adequacy is available, and even more so, for the future. From this knowledge we realize that we have developed courage by facing seemingly unsurmountable opposition and overcoming it, that we have developed patience by not getting our way immediately, that we have come by tolerance by living quietly in nearly intolerable circumstances, and that we have been content even when we were not satisfied.

It is impossible to describe joy to the person who has never felt it, and for the person who has felt it, description is totally inadequate—even unnecessary. Joy is seldom as effervescent as happiness or as transient. It does not come from the outside but wells up from the inside. It is a value; not just something to be valued. It has a relationship with happiness, just as flirtation has a relationship with love, but happiness never goes as deep as joy.

For example, a young man may thoroughly enjoy dating various girls, singing "There ain't nothing like a dame" with every flirtation. He is happy, but then life changes when he meets one girl with whom he does more than flirt—he falls in love. Now going out with different girls is no longer a thrill because he only wants to go out with one girl. The many girls who used to entice him now simply remind him that he is not with the one girl he loves. He is sad where once he was glad. What once was exciting is now depressing.

This is the relationship between joy and happiness. Joy is the deep, settled satisfaction that keeps returning to feed our life and spirit. It enables us somehow, even while we are covered over by the everlasting demands, to feel that we are undergirded by the everlasting arms.

The Divine Quality

Finally, *joy has a divine quality* about it; therefore it needs to be connected to the eternal. One of our friends has been working with young people in one of our neighborhoods where the young executive fathers are constantly moving. He notices that these kids have real trouble relating to others on any deep and meaningful basis, for they have learned not to put down roots which will be yanked out when the family moves. He has found that relating them to the eternal provides a system of roots that helps in their relating on a temporary basis.

When we feel that time is simply the "entrance ramp" to eternity, it gives us a feeling of continuity. This life becomes the practice, and the next life becomes the game. Whichever we believe to be the game or the practice is extremely important, for so often we play this life as if it were the game, not understanding much of the drudgery and discipline of practice. When we understand life as the practice with the game coming later, we even accomplish some joy in the practice by anticipating the joy of the game.

Often football players say, "Only on Sunday in the game does the practice become really worthwhile."

Christians who try to live the Christian life without the indwelling Spirit fail to exude joy. They are like people going on a trip with so much baggage that they enlarge the storage capacity of the car by removing the engine. The Spirit is our "engine," and when the engine goes, the joy goes.

Beware the unbalanced life, for it is often the joyless life. The Mayo Clinic announced a new cure for getting over the "tired feeling" by showing the patients how to live a balanced life. Dr. Richard Clark Cabot gave the formula: work, play, love, and worship. And the Mayo Clinic made a cross of four arms of equal length to represent the ideal life. This is the life in which there can be resident joy.

Joy has a price. It does not come cheap or by chance. It comes through discipline. "Let not your heart be troubled" is a command, not a suggestion. This is good news, for joy comes by process, not by accident. This process we can learn and practice—and have joy for the journey.

THINK ABOUT IT . . .

As we make the best of the present, we insure the joy of the future.

Among the strong, the elimination of happiness often intensifies joy.

The invisible is most clearly seen by the eyes of a good heart.

Love is the only sanity—a world in love would be at peace.

Joy cannot be contained—it must be shared.

When joy overflows your cup, try spilling it on someone.

"The Spirit produces love, joy, peace, patience, kindness, goodness, faithfulness, humility, and self-control." Galatians 5:22

If fear makes us tough, we are wrong; but if love makes us tough, we are right.

II

THE PEOPLE
IN
YOUR NETWORK

Your friends, heroes, mentors—even your enemies—are vital links in exciting living.

THE PEOPLE
IN YOUR NETWORK

Introduction

Networking is the way most things happen and, even though it is a fairly new term, it's an old, old idea. Great achievers have always understood the necessity of organized assistance.

Ancient dynasties, empires, and kingdoms were supported by intermarriage networks, for they knew that blood was thicker than water. Successful businesses have depended on building the network between suppliers, customers, government agencies, stockholders, employees, and management.

The human body, probably the oldest network, has many parts—each connected to the other through nerves and blood vessels, muscle and bone. The foot depends on the eyes to keep it from stumbling, just as the eye depends on the eyebrow to keep the sweat from running into it.

Through the right use of networking we can find a smoother and more sure route to the abundant life Christ came to provide. As we are willing to serve others, others are anxious to repay our service. Do unto others as you would have them do unto you, but be sure you do it first—start the good.

Networking helps us enjoy the riches of our opportunity.

It can be the *modus operandi* of success. When we create a healthy relation to others, we are not alone in a jungle, and we can be assured life is worth living.

Successful networking isn't an accident. It just doesn't happen. For some, using the network is intuitive, but most of us have to learn to use our network constructively. It isn't enough to say, "It's who you know, not what you know." It is both who you know and what you know. When Emerson said, "Build a better mousetrap and the world will beat a path to your door," he only understood half the truth. Many a good mousetrap has gone unnoticed and the inventor unrewarded. Good ideas have to find a market, just as capable individuals have to be recognized, and this requires networking.

If no one has told you how it works, then I want to tell you in plain, simple, practical, workable language. When you succeed, I will succeed, for vicariously I will share your accomplishment and fulfill my aim in life to be one who stretches others.

Here is the way I have experienced it.

1

YOU

The Person You Mean to Be

Dear You:

If you are a contributing person, or sincerely want to be, this chapter is for you. For you are the most important part of your Power Network which exists to support you.

Here are practical, proven principles which have helped others succeed in life and living, and these same benefits are available to you in your lifetime climb.

We have come through a time when ne'er-do-wells, particularly young ones, have been saying, "Love me for myself." So often that remark is similar to the one in the store, "Buy as is." Generally the item is broken or won't work.

A person should only ask to be loved for themselves when they are making something lovable out of themselves. The Allan Emerys of Boston took a young girl into their home. She had lost her way in life. After dinner each evening, Allan would go through a series of questions with her by which she was learning to live again. The first question was, "Why does God love you?" To which she replied, "Not because I am good, but because I am precious." Then he would ask, "Why are you precious?" To which she would reply, "Because Christ loved me enough to die for me." Even if you have lost your dignity, you have not lost your preciousness. If you want to be a better somebody, no matter where you are now, you can do it.

This chapter is for *you.*

Sincerely,
Fred Smith

I believe in working for success much more than praying for it. Pray for maturity and work for success. If your success comes with your maturity, you will know best how to use it, how to enjoy it, and how to perpetuate it. As you work for success, work enthusiastically, work intelligently, work intensely, and work ethically.

A friend wrote this reminder on his wall: "A thing that needs doing can be done honestly." If it can't be done honestly, then it doesn't need doing. Honest goals have honest means and methods available. Finding the right means will at times strain your creativity but not your morals. It's still the same old story: Good ends never launder dirty means.

Get Yourself a Clear Definition of Success

There are several useful definitions, but money alone, to me, is not one of them. "Success is using your talents and gifts to their highest advantage and contribution. Wealth may come with this, or it may not." Martha Friedman, psychiatrist, defines internal success as "getting to do what you really want to do in your work life and in your love life, doing it very well and feeling good about yourself doing it."

My associate Joe Dominy gave me this one: "Something to do, someone to love, something to look forward to."

Another simple one: "Optimum use of talents and opportunities for the good of others, including self." As Rotary puts it: "He profits most who serves best." /

Clarify Your Philosophical Base

Behind every plan of action, every commitment of time and energy, should be a solid philosophical base. From it comes our answer to "why?" Why should I be a leader? Why should I pay the price of success? Why not stay where it is comfortable? Why push ahead, risking failure? Is it just for ego, or do I feel I have been given a talent, an opportunity, and I don't want to miss the excitement of worthwhile accomplishment in any period of life, whether youth, middle age, or older years?

Your reason for moving up will have little to do with how far you go. It will, however, have a great deal to do with your mental and spiritual attitude as you go. The folks closest to you will see, feel, and be affected most by this.

Often when I am with friends who have become "successful" but unhappy, I feel they are proof of the verse in Psalms which says, "And he gave them their request, but sent leanness into their soul." Such people are constantly irritated, never enjoying the fruits of success, always moving on as if goaded by the spirit of their discontent, always coming to the truth but never really finding it. They have no quiet center for their lives . . . No eye of the storm in which they can lie down and sleep until the activity starts again. They live in "quiet desperation" while longing for the "quiet adequacy"—a time for enjoying their options provided by their success and/or wealth.

More common than the "leanness of soul" is the boredom that comes with "leveling off"—a phenomenon I see so many executives and professionals repeatedly suffer after quickly rising in their careers. Suddenly they flatten out where they stay for the remainder of their careers. Why don't they go higher?

This is the only explanation I know. At first, young people new on the job are full of physical energy. In a new ball game, they are excited. They respond—with great effort and desire—to the feel of competition for promotion. They move ahead until the fire of physical energy starts to level out at about age forty or so. They then begin to seek their "comfort" level. To push on, they will need a nonphysical spiritual drive that overcomes the temptation of comfort. If there is none, they live out their lives near this same level.

Life is a two-stage rocket. The first is physical energy—it ignites and we are off. As physical energy diminishes, the spiritual stage must ignite to boost us into orbit or we fall back or plateau.

There are two kinds of spiritual (nonphysical) energy: ego and responsibility. Productively, I cannot differentiate between the two. Generally the production is about equal. But the spirit is remarkably different. Running on ego alone hardens or destroys a person—like a machine without oil, there is a terrible increase in friction, often followed by burnout. On the other hand, a sense of responsibility gives great energy—a uniting force which pulls the person together, not apart. It protects the machine—the faster the speed, the greater value the lubrication of responsibility. There is joy in the going.

Choose a Direction with Intermediate Goals—
It's the Direction That Counts

Choosing a goal in life is not our most important decision. Choosing the direction is more important than choosing the goal. Enticing short-range goals can take us in the wrong direction. Mature success and satisfaction come in the direction we move, not in the goals we attain.

Too much goal orientation brings us the same problem that Harvard Business School found in the case system of teaching, where bright young students learned to solve problems rather than to identify opportunities. The real progress in life comes in recognizing opportunities. Problem-solving is important, but it is just a means of taking advantage of the opportunities.

When we become too goal-oriented, we become almost technological and mechanical in our approach to life. Who wants to be a computer—even a human computer?

I oppose setting an ultimate goal for one's life, in the sense of a specific, definable, measurable, figure-oriented, or describable place in life at which one hopes ultimately to arrive. This puts too much importance on one decision which, many times, cannot be made properly. This creates futility in those who reach what they have termed success and find it was attaining the goal and not the goal itself they really enjoyed. They are then left in the "yellow leaf" of life, like the man who assiduously climbed the ladder only to find that it was leaning against the wrong building.

Goals are mainly important to confirm that we are traveling in the direction we intended to go.

I prefaced my decision as to what direction I wanted by visiting a graveyard. While sitting on a tombstone I thought about what really is important in life. We know many presidents have been driven by how history will remember them. In a sense all of us have a history in which we would like to be remembered favorably. It may not be published, outside a few family members and friends, or it may be simply a name in a family Bible—but it is our life and we have the opportunity to decide to a great degree how we are going to live it.

When young people ask me for advice on finding a direction for life, I start out by asking if they want to be "useful" or "self-fulfilled." As long as they see these two as opposites, it is going to be difficult for them to take a mature view of life. I have never known a truly useful person who didn't feel fulfilled. I have never known a miserable person who was unselfishly giving to others. There is a great truth in the paradox that a lost life is a found life.

When I chose my own direction for life, I also chose a mythical epitaph for my tombstone: "He stretched others."

As an executive, I enjoyed seeing people productive and growing.

Once, serving on a board of directors with Mason Roberts, then president of Frigidaire, I was inspired by his thought, "When you get a hundred individuals to do 1 percent more than they would have done without you, you have created a new life." As I think back on my many years in executive life, I can repeat with Maxey Jarman what he said to me near his retirement, "It's not the many plants we've built, but the many people we have developed which is my greatest satisfaction."

Planning Is Important

Each January 1st I go to the office and work out a detailed inventory and review of last year's plan and a projection of the coming year. Beside the things I have accomplished I put a plus; beside the things I have failed to accomplish I put a minus. Those which I decided during the year were not really do-able or worthwhile I "x" out. Such a discipline is particularly helpful to someone not under close supervision, such as myself.

Much of this I say to show my respect for setting goals, but only secondarily, for primarily I believe in setting a direction. This has been my direction: "To define a lifestyle and then earn enough money to support it." In defining the lifestyle, I took into consideration my best talents, the contribution I felt was my responsibility to make to life, and the total effect these had on the organization, my relations with family and close friends.

I always considered the variable of the opportunities at hand and the times. Timing is always so important.

Work the Plan

Our intermediate goals give us specific opportunities for planning. Therefore, we must concentrate on the immediate goal enough to develop a plan that will accomplish it.

Many years ago, when I was doing a series of business lectures in Chicago, a young Paul Meyer came from Florida to spend the day with me. It was a memorable day for me and, I hope, helpful for him. He showed me his plan for success, which he has certainly followed. One of the features I adopted into my own thinking: *Set the goal, then forget it and concentrate on working the plan enthusiastically.*

Most of us can become very enthusiastic about goals, for they define for us benefits. But few of us can really be enthusiastic about the plan of work for reaching the goal. For example, a fat person is delighted with the goal of losing twenty-five pounds but is much less enthusiastic about the plan called a diet. The fat comes off by working the plan, not setting the goal. A salesperson can be enthusiastic about earning an extra five thousand dollars this year—but much less enthusiastic about making an extra call a day. The apostle Paul understood this quirk and learned to stay enthusiastic about the detailed plan he had developed for reaching the goal.

Select a Pleasant Route

Too often, after we select our destination and make our plans, we fail to look at all the possible ways of getting there. Recently, on the West Coast, I decided to turn off the interstate and follow an exciting scenic route. Generally we miss the byways and endure the interstates to "save time." Is time always that important? Sometimes we have our goal so much in mind that we fail to take another, more leisurely, interesting way. I am saying that both the destination and the route should be considered, and both should be interesting. We spend a great deal more time on the road than we do at the destination. Therefore, pick the best road, which isn't always the fastest. Learn how to enjoy the whole trip, the road as well as the goal.

I must illustrate by telling about one dear friend with whom I rode through Switzerland in the summer. As we left each hotel, he would ask the concierge how long it should take us to get to the next town. Being a very competitive person, he determined to beat the time by at least fifteen minutes. He did, by going so fast I needed a movie camera in the window so I could review it in slow motion and see where we had been. We must have passed some very interesting places, but we went by them so quickly they remain a blur.

I used to do this same thing with family trips in the car. I was so time- and schedule-oriented that I would set our travel plan by our expected MPH rather than points of interest. Our sensible kids were not overly enthusiastic about traveling that way. I've seen so many persons speeding through life hoping to get to a destination which they really are not going to enjoy after they get there. Some unfortunate friends delayed enjoying life until "retirement"—and then it was too late. They were out of health or death cancelled their plans. Be sure you make the going pleasant as well as the arriving. Plan the route as carefully as you do the destination.

Don't Forget the Money

I never minimized the necessity of financing my way of life, but I always wanted money to be a means and never an end. I've had some unfortunate examples among my friends who totally dedicated themselves to making money and then tried to find a way to live in between the money-making events. With those who do so knowingly, I have no argument. However, most of them seemed to slip into this rut, becoming entangled and enmeshed in "materialism." Making money is such an urgent affair.

In American society money looms so large I have included in this chapter a separate section entitled "Money and Your Peace of Mind."

Take Control of Your Time

Personally I've never been pressured for lack of time. In fact, I've never had a job that used my full time except for short stretches, and I was very self-conscious—even guilty—about this until I met a brilliant, successful CEO (chief executive officer) of a multi-billion-dollar corporation. He confided one night that he, too, had never found enough that was exclusively his in a job to stay busy eight hours, all day, every day. This admission horrifies most people because I have a sneaking feeling that they really feel that as leaders and gung-ho achievers they are supposed to be pressured by lack of time.

As a heretic against time pressure, I at least will support my position by stating a concept or philosophy about the utilization of time. As a very modest accomplisher, I have no right to feel that I don't have enough time so long as the greats of the world have done everything they've done in the same twenty-four hours that I have. Yet small, as well as great, accomplishers grouse over lack of time. Time pressure is a modern fad—almost an American fad.

Another part of my concept is that time is personal—just as personal as money. If you do not let other people indiscriminately spend your money, you have no obligation to let them spend your time. Your time, like your money, is yours to spend and to control.

Time, like money, varies in value. High energy hours, like after-tax dollars, are more productive and therefore more valuable.

In considering organization of time, here are the things I feel are important:

1. *Decide specifically what you're trying to do.* When I list the things in my job that only I can do, it can become an embarrassingly short list. Anything that anyone else can do as well or better, I am in the process of giving over to them—first by assignment, then by delegation. It

requires ego control to accept how many people can do
most of what we think we have to do—and do it better.

2. *Keep a reasonably heavy schedule of meaningful things that
really count.* Work pace is important. When the pace is too
fast, we make haphazard decisions and get our priorities
confused. If the pace is too slow, we have a tendency to
procrastinate even more, letting Parkinson's Law take over.
Most people do their best, productive work in the week
before their vacation. They make decisions, they get things
done, because they have to.

3. *Learn to use small bits of time.* Successful people use
small bits of time better than the less successful. It isn't
the large chunks of time that make the winning difference.
The large demands on time fall about the same for most
of us. The scraps of wasted time are where the winning
edge is. For example, I have noticed that generally the
most successful individuals leave a meeting first.

4. *Be organized—orderly or not.* The delightful writer Elisa-
beth Elliott asked my wife if I were orderly. I couldn't
take a chance on her answer (for I am not), so I said defen-
sively, "I'm not orderly, but I am organized." Orderliness
is a pleasant trait but organization is a necessity.

Knowing how to use bits of time is an art. Evelyn Nelson,
partner of the Russell Stover Candy Co., carried a note-
sized pad and wrote short letters to her friends and business associates when she had "waiting time." I adopted
her idea. Robert Turner, retired president of Genuine
Parts, has a TV in his sauna for watching the news. Time-
savers learn to comfortably combine routine activities.

One of the most practical suggestions I could make to
corporations in time control would be to deduct the expenses of every meeting called by an executive from his
bonus. I am being facetious—but not totally. This happened to me when I left a large corporation and formed
my own company. When the money was coming out of
my pocket it was surprising how few meetings we really
needed.

For those serious about saving or better utilizing time

(since we can't really save it without getting Joshua to stop the sun), I suggest you make a list of only five ways to improve your use of time and then practice them until they become second nature. Better to practice five than learn ten we don't use.

Maintain a Development Program

> "Reading makes a full man."
> —Francis Bacon

Do you live in a neighborhood of truly interesting people, even great ones? If not, would you like to? You can when you surround yourself with the books these people have written—and those written about them. Better to read their books than to talk with them, for their writing is more carefully thought out than their casual conversation could ever be. Would you like to talk with Einstein? Then open a book of his essays. Had you rather listen to Emerson? He is in the library at your convenience. If you long to be a more complete thinker, then you must read the Bible, as the vast majority of great thinkers have done whether they believed or not. Do you need courage? Then read the second most read book ever written—*Pilgrim's Progress*. Or you might want to know more about human nature. Is there a better source than Shakespeare? If you are in the mood for profitable entertainment, then you have all the choice in the world. Reward yourself with the company of the greats or the pleasantness of the interesting, those who have written as they probed the secrets of science, traveled to remote places, thought the great thoughts, or watched the human parade pass their vantage point. Join them and be blessed.

A Warm Word for Personal Letters

Perhaps I have written a few thousand personal letters in my life. No, I am not exaggerating, for letter writing is my joy and curse. Yet I *think* more letters than I *write*, for I dislike meaningless letters written for courtesy only, saying, "My good manners say I should say something but I don't have anything to say to you." Friends should understand quiet as the rest notes of their harmony.

"Smith's night letters" are written from a continuous roll of paper fed through my typewriter on which with two fingers I follow the scriptural instruction, "seek and ye shall find." Sometimes a friend gets a two-inch letter; others might be weighted down with one three feet long.

While I have very few copies from all these years of letter writing, I do have great memories of those rambling personal epistles:

To: Bill Mead, my long-time friend and benefactor.

To: Howard Butt, Jr., who let me ride his spiritual back until I had strength enough to stand.

To: Our children, who were more friends than children.

To: College students like Ed, who signed his letter, "Until I hear from you I'll be floating around."

To: Young musicians, encouragement in the talent they had which I wanted but never had.

To: Maxey Jarman, the man of great character and accomplishment.

To: Dr. Julian Gumperz, whose New York obituary read, "The awesome intellect of Julian Gumperz is gone," but it isn't so long as his friends survive in his great spirit of intellectual integrity.

To: A brother in the Marines, fighting on Guadalcanal on Christmas day.

To: Lonely friends going through death's valley hoping for a star in their night.

To: Friends who have failed and are tempted to stay down for the count.

To: Friends who have succeeded wildly and now wonder who they can trust.

To: Frank, the penitentiary lifer writing music in solitary, needing to trust someone for the music to be heard.

To: A friend who needed his rear kicked for repeating a mistake I too had made.

To: A friendly critic who cared enough to read, reread, and react constructively.

To: My courageous mother who liked for the neighbors to see her receive mail from her son.

Association

("Association makes a broader man")

Most association just happens. I think there's a better way. Association should be planned. The truism, "Birds of a feather flock together," is not always the best formula for profitable, purposeful association. Those who want to be eagles can't spend all their time with turkeys.

One of the most touching stories I know involves a janitor in our executive offices, a most accommodating man of sterling character. He originally had a job out in the plant and asked to be transferred to the executive offices as janitor. Because he lacked education, he knew he could not get to be even a clerical worker. But he had several children and felt that if he were a janitor among the executives, from time to time his children would get to meet and know them. This contact, he felt, would give them a vision of being as much as they could. This made me greatly respect this man, even more than I respected several of the executives. He used association for the right reason.

I grew up in a neighborhood where you got a job, stayed with it, married, and raised your family in the same neighborhood. One's children were expected to repeat the process. Those who moved up and out were not really appreciated. They were thought of as "uppity"—and those who had any taste for culture or literature were considered odd. The boys grew up to be young men, played neighborhood softball, volleyball, and so forth; when they got too old for these, they started bowling, which they did for the rest of their lives. One of the main objectives in finding a job was to find one with a good retirement program.

I recall one of the older men in our neighborhood "dressing me down" for not wanting to go to work as a mail carrier and enjoy the government's good retirement program. That was the basic mentality of the group in which I grew up. Many of them are the salt of the earth, with deep motivation to stay in the group and no desire to move out. Desire to move up was breaking rank. This social caste system keeps a great many locked in.

Two of the greatest organizations I know for youth are Youth for Christ and Young Life. They offer young people in high school who are serious about life an alternative peer group—one that is constructive, healthy, positive.

We refer to young people as being malleable, or formable. We recognize the importance of their peer groups in their growth process. However, it has been my experience that we adults can stay malleable and pliable our entire life if we choose. Those who pick a peer group and become concretized usually do so because they do not consider alternatives. We impose a caste system on ourselves. Our upward mobility is, for most, simply a matter of economics, not of culture, literature, intelligence, spiritual growth, or leadership. Yet these are the areas where we need upward mobility.

I have had a simple growth formula for myself: "Try to be the smallest person in the group." It's tough on the ego but once you've learned to handle that problem, you are very appreciative of the opportunity to grow into your association with others—not just in money, but all the other traits of life which we have available to us.

We associate up to learn and associate down to teach. It is difficult to lift another unless you are above him. Being above him increases our responsibility to lift. This keeps us operating in two groups—those from whom we are learning and those whom we are teaching. The wonderful thing about our human flexibility is that we can keep growing our whole life through.

How to Choose Associates

Character is the foundation upon which worthwhile accomplishments must be built. Fortunately, through association we can build our better foundation with people of strong character who are in all levels, social and economic, of our society.

Positive Traits through Association

1. *Integrity*—Wherein a person is consistent in trying to do what is right.

2. *Love of truth*—Scholars are honored for their "search for truth." But we all must search, for truth is not always on the surface. It helps, however, to be in the company of those who want and respect truth. In a small mill section of Nashville, in a three-room row house, I met one of the great characters of my life. Mrs. Carter worked for as little as two dollars and fifty cents a week and raised her children after her husband had deserted her during the Depression. You could count on Mrs. Carter; she told the truth. Her friendship personified truth and integrity. She was not a scholar; she was a saint in the slums. I suppose about the only thing she read was her favorite parts of the Bible—but she loved truth and personified it to me. I am better for having known her.

3. *Unselfishness*—I have never known a person of strong character whose first thought was, "What's in it for me?" This idea lies at the heart of greed. It bespeaks an animal world where the fittest survive and where caring for another is weakness rather than strength.

4. *Decisiveness*—Maxey Jarman and I were crossing Fifth Avenue at Fifty-seventh Street just before he retired as chairman of Genesco. He was reminiscing about his business experience, which he very rarely did, but this evening he said, "I am convinced that the rarest trait in the executive life is decisiveness." Ultimate leadership demands decisiveness. And it helps to associate with decisive individuals.

5. *Courage*—Only those who have faced problems—possibly defeat—know whether they have courage. Courage is not living in the fantasy of fiction; it is living in the turmoil of life. Courage overcomes panic. It gives us the ability to concentrate by thinking of the right thing at the right time. It has the ability to stand against odds and to think under pressure.

I read "Little Orphan Annie" many years ago, but I remember very well something Daddy Warbucks said: "A coward dies many times, a brave man only once." I thought of that the day I was riding through Montgomery, Alabama, listening to the radio in my car. They were loading the first bus in the Black Rights Movement. A middle-aged black woman was being interviewed on the radio. Asked how she felt, she replied, "I *think* I'm going to be scared, but I *know* I'm not." Inside her was a heart of courage. Much of courage is centered in our will. The general getting ready to ride into battle noticed that his knees were shaking and he said to them, "Shake, will you? If you knew where I'm going to take you today, you would tremble." Courage commands the fear which is in all of us.

6. *Graciousness*—Graciousness is more than good manners—it is more than courtesy—it is the etiquette of the soul. True graciousness has such a divine quality we feel it is something that comes through us and not from us.

I first met Grant and Orean Howard when speaking to a national convention of office equipment manufacturers. We were having dinner in the Conrad Hilton and almost immediately I sensed Orean's great gift of graciousness.

Her "hello" was a blessing more than a greeting. When she asked "How are you?" it was with the concern of someone who cared—someone who would be happy to listen. Shortly, in a rather facetious way, I commented, "Orean, with a wife as gracious as you, I can understand why Grant is president of the association." Without any false surprise or humble facade, she replied, "Fred, thank you for noticing my graciousness. I have dedicated it to Jesus Christ." I was so taken aback by that remark that I, of a skeptical nature, decided to visit them in their home just to evaluate this a little more.

Early the first morning, I walked into the living room and saw this lady standing by the window with the bright sunshine of Phoenix coming through. Not knowing anyone else was in the house, I mistakenly thought it was Orean. I spoke to her, calling her Orean, and the lady turned around and said, "Thank you for calling me by my mother's name. I couldn't be more honored."

I'm not sure how much of graciousness is a gift and how much is a developed trait, but I am sure of one thing: All of us can improve, and while we might not near perfection, we can be so much more gracious than we are inclined to be that others will be grateful for our improvement. Association helps.

Keep Your Sense of Humor

I must say that I was surprised, though actually delighted, to find that Plato looked down on, even demeaned, humor. Though I did not hear him say it directly, it has been reported to me that he felt it was immature. A society with a philosopher with such opinion of humor is bound to have eclipsed. I'm surprised it lasted as long as it did. In forgiveness, we can humor his idiosyncrasy and still remember him as one of the great thinkers—for we know that not even they are perfect. But they would have been more perfect with a sense of good humor!

Humor is the true measure of our humanity. Without it, we are handicapped personalities, incapable of reaching our utmost possibilities. Only an I.Q. of our humor, if one existed, could tell us how truly and thoroughly human we are. Until one comes, we can enjoy ourselves, believing we are humor geniuses.

The great physicist Edward Teller, writing about his favorite pipe-dream, wishes computers might learn to write jokes. This he believes they can do if we can precisely define one—which, of course, he points out, we can't. Therein is the charm and usefulness of humor. Humor is safe from technology. We can laugh at it, but it can't laugh at us. While technology can foul us up, it can't make fun of us.

Writers of biography, of both the worthy and unworthy, invariably give us an evaluation of their subject's "sense of humor" or lack of it. Magazine and newspaper writers often keep the person's sense of humor until last, using it as the crowning or redeeming quality. They justify the high and mighty by giving them a kindly sense of humor to connect their eliteness to our mediocrity. Even criminals doing dastardly things, possessing few good qualities, are finally spared complete castigation by being endowed with a touch of humor. If one made a humorous remark on the way to the gallows it would automatically become the headline of his execution: "He died laughing."

A sense of humor, like attitude, is impossible to precisely define. We can say general things, such as "humor makes us laugh," but good humor doesn't always laugh—sometimes it only smiles and then again it merely helps us to see things more pleasantly, enduring the hurt until health returns.

When properly mixed with the other chemistry of our feelings, humor promotes a continual sense of well-being. It adds strength to our character and sweetness to our personality, starting from the inside, like a genuine smile, working its way out onto our face.

Humor is an expression of our philosophy, coming even more from the heart than the mind. King David saw it as having medicinal value and said, "A merry heart doeth good like a medicine."

Humor rose-tints the potential of life without losing the objective present. This ability, like a sense of intelligence or moral rightness, is always expandable. Therefore, it's important that all areas of life be permeated with a healthy humor.

Money and Your Peace of Mind

Many have a profound ability to let misuse and misunderstanding of money sour all their relationships and severely limit their growth. I want to talk frankly about money and how it contributes to peace of mind because money is important to you.

Venita VanCaspel, president of VanCaspel Company in Houston, is hostess of the highly successful TV program, "Winning the Money Game." I was her first guest and also appeared twice on her TV show, "Successful Texans." In her excellent best seller, *The Power of Money Dynamics,* she inscribed her book to me: "To my dear friend Fred Smith who has won the money game and many others." I feel immodest in telling this, but I make no apologies for exploring this "crass subject." I am interested in "winning the money game," and there is no reason why you shouldn't build on a solid set of principles, too.

For years I have seriously studied money. Yet I don't fully know what money is. It is more than a "medium of exchange"—it is an influence. It is a power—a symbol. For some unfortunate few it is an idol. To Americans, money, like love, is its own reason for being . . . its own explanation. Money is a common denominator for so many things that so many want. It is the meeting point for our mind's desires, hopes, aspirations, and even sense of security. Money grows in the heart before it grows in the pocket. Granted, money does not provide everything, but give it credit; it does have an aura that makes people believe it provides more than any other one thing! Money is probably our Number 1 motivator.

There are hundreds of books on how to make money, how to spend it, and how to keep it. However, none satisfactorily explains the true meaning of money.

The people we read of in the Old Testament thought their material possessions confirmed God's favor toward them. Many of the Puritans, who considered America the New Jerusalem and Americans the new chosen of God, viewed money as evidence of a special relationship with God. Not only do I not believe that, but I blush for those who do. I am troubled when I think of saints in poverty having to bear this additional judgment from some who deem their money to be a reward from God when, in fact, they have fortuitously been at the right place at the right time. It is incredible to suggest that God highly favors in a special way the infinitesimally small group that have acquired wealth in the Christian community. Even overzealous speakers claim that God wants everyone whom he can trust to be rich. They insinuate most people are poor because God can't trust them. Pitiful arrogance! Money is not God's reward for his saints.

I have suffered the disadvantages of poverty, even as I now know the limitations of wealth. The sin of the poor is envy, while the sin of the wealthy is greed. Yet I believe greed is more productive than envy. Envy produces little or nothing, while greed often spins the productive wheel, enriching the greedy who may eventually pass some along to others as wages or gifts.

This is my best definition: "Money is option." Money brings options, just as poverty eliminates them. While money provides options, it does not supply the ability to choose the right option. That requires character.

As a young man I had little or no money; my options

were restricted. Today young people control amazing amounts of money and with it multiply their options. Possibly this is one of the biggest differences between the generations.

Some well-meaning, though inadequate, thinkers decry money per se. They fail to realize the value of well-used options. Slaves have few options, but this doesn't mean their lives cannot be beneficial. In the German concentration camp Viktor Frankl had few options, but he used the ones he had. He slept less, he hated less, he brooded less, and he used his time to develop his theory of Logotherapy.

Later, with money available, he was able to finance his writings and bless the world.

Aleksandr Solzhenitsyn in Siberia was without the usual civilized options, but he took advantage of the few he had and was later able to bless "that stinking straw." He didn't purposely eliminate his options; he simply concentrated on the few left to him until he gained more. Today he lives comfortably.

Paucity builds a discipline of choice; it encourages one to choose well from limited choices. These principles of proper choice can and should be carried over into the value system when money options become available.

The Optional Society

America talks about its mobile society, when in reality it is an optional society. We are an affluent society as well as a democratic one, with choices. This is where the rubber marks the road. Money is a means, made good or bad by our choice of option.

Writing in *The Mature Society,* Dr. Dennis Gabor questions why there has never been a rich society that has lived very long. In adversity he found societies could prove strong, virile, even noble, while in periods of affluence they became decadent, selfish, and eventually extinct.

Often it takes character to handle poverty, but more

character to handle affluence. A few do very noble things with money. Most of us are not made proud by our choices but, rather, become proud of our possessions.

Money Disciplines

A few early money disciplines served me well—and naturally I suggest these or similar ones for consideration. I adopted these when I was making $208 per month in 1941. Mary Alice and I had married in 1937 with five dollars between us. Really, it was her five dollars. I jokingly tell her if she thinks that we should have had more money when we married, then she should have saved more.

1. *Define a lifestyle, then find a way to finance it.* Earning as much money as I could never seemed to be the right focus for life. Money was a means that was to be swapped for something else. Some advise: "Make all you can and then develop a lifestyle to consume the money." That is materialism. It's also frustrating, and very few who have adopted this philosophy really feel they are living a meaningful life.

Mary Alice and I defined a general lifestyle spread over a number of years that would be useful, pleasant, and full. With this framework we then established the specifics each year. This included our current living expenses, savings, provision for the children's education, and some money for family development through travel, education, and culture as well as social contacts. It also included religious and charitable giving which, we felt, was a requirement for our well-being. We put a reasonably specific budget onto this and came up with an annual earnings figure which was adequate to finance it. That living wage kept me from falling into the trap of accepting just any job which paid more. With a definite amount specified, I could feel that I was making a satisfactory income and not be eternally looking for "more," never satisfied that I was making enough.

As our earning capacity increased, we continued defining the lifestyle first, including some luxuries, but not enough to live luxuriously. We wanted to avoid the pressures and temptations. For example, during the children's early life we did not belong to the country club, not because it was particularly wrong, but we just felt we wanted a little more control in the family. Later we joined, when we felt the children were capable of handling it.

One of the temptations, of course, is to "keep up with the Joneses." We were perfectly willing for the Joneses to have anything they wanted. Sticking to our definition of our lifestyle we were able to determine our own course without competing with them. For forty-six years we have lived with this concept and would do it all over again.

2. *Maintain adequate savings.* Early in our married life, we determined to save at least enough liquid assets to live for one year without working. Without savings a person can become a financial slave. It cost us some early hardship to get this savings, because we had to do without a car and live in a one-room flat, but we've never regretted it.

Adequate savings gives more than just a feeling of security. It actually provides a foundation for any moral decisions you are called upon to make in business. Only once was I faced with such a moral decision. I was vice president, and the board knew I could not be financially pressured. This gave me the latitude to take a moral stand which eventually came out well for all of us. I am convinced that if I could not have stood financially, it would have been much more difficult to take the stand, even though it was moral. It is a tough decision to put a job on the line when we cannot face next month's bills. This reserve fund has kept me from having that onerous experience.

Recently a friend whose annual income is now into seven figures brought me a piggy bank from Mexico with hand-inscribed letters, "FFGTHF." The minute I looked at it we both broke up laughing. I remembered what the letters stood for, and I remembered that I had given him the thought several years before. It had been helpful to him. The letters on that piggy bank stood for: "Fat Fred's Go-to-H—— Fund." That was what, in my early, more rebellious years, I originally called my savings account. Now I refer to it in a mild sort of "go take a long leap." However, if he had to remember the earlier words to remember the principle, I guess that ameliorates it considerably.

3. *Define "financial security" at a definite figure.* Security is a feeling, not a fact. No amount of money can actually give us security, and yet one needs a feeling of financial security which can be extremely helpful in making good decisions. By setting a specific figure we can develop a plan for getting there and develop habits which we can review at that time. So many people develop habits early in life and never review them or change them as their circumstances change.

Before we reached our specific goal, our emphasis was on savings. After we reached it, we let up on savings and tried to spend wisely, doing the things we had saved our money to do. A Canadian friend, who became president of an insurance company there, discovered that he was working night and day. He wasn't really sure why. As he reviewed his life, he realized that he had been born very poor. Thus he wanted to do a lot of things during his life which would take money. He developed his habit of working very hard and saving all he could. He was now making the money but not doing the things he had intended to use the money for. He talked to his board of directors and worked out a most unusual arrangement: he would continue heading the corporation but would only work six months out of the year. He felt it was senseless to make the money and not get to do the things that he was making the money to do. Often people save and delay all of their expectations until they reach a certain age. At that time too often some of them are dead and others don't have the health to really enjoy what they had planned to do.

Unfortunately, sometimes, people get so enamored of their habits that they change the "security" amount just so they can keep following their old habit pattern. Learning to spend money wisely is just as difficult as becoming an habitual saver.

After Mary Alice and I reached our goal, we continued to save, but secondarily. Primarily we spend on investments, development, travel, gifts, and the like. It is sad when people who are able to do things don't. Instead they only collect memories of what they intend to do rather than what they did. Of course, money habits must change with the conditions; therefore, the conditions should be specifically defined and anticipated. Inflation can change specific amounts.

Since money has such a strange hold on us, I think it might be helpful to tell this story as a warning. A young, successful man brought me his financial statement, which was comfortably into the millions. He asked my advice on his getting into a business deal which could easily make him ten times as wealthy. It was a highly speculative venture, a sort of Russian roulette in the money game.

I asked what he and his family could do with ten times the money that they couldn't now do with the millions they already had. I was trying to smoke out his ego without hurting his feelings. Yet I didn't feel that I could urge him not to make a decision which might make him a very wealthy man. However, I did feel the responsibility to give him a rule which had guided my thinking while my family was young: "I have no need to be extremely rich—but I have a great need not to be broke."

I would not take speculations which would materially change our family's lifestyle, I told him. I have never felt I was justified in gambling my family's future just to make excessive amounts of money. It might be nice to be envied in the business community or at the club—but it's just too dangerous for the family. He understood my point but disagreed—and went ahead into tragic bankruptcy. I feel more for his family than for him. The children are suffering at a time in their lives when the family should be solid and secure.

The Basic Philosophy

As you can see, what I have been basically talking about is maintaining control of one's life. It is much easier to make moral decisions when there is no financial pressure. Money is a means and not an end. Money is important, just as important as blood, but we make blood to live; we don't live to make blood.

I'm always curious when I see someone obviously living to make money. I suspect that maybe they have figured out a way to go through this life twice. The first time through they're going to make the money, and the second time through they're going to spend it. I'm not that wise— and so I'm going to have to make and spend it my only time through.

Giving

Giving is part of life and should start whenever our financial life starts. One must not wait until he makes big money to start giving. Few men who wait to give ever really give. Giving is part of building a whole life. My dear friend Maxey Jarman had given millions of dollars to Christian causes. In the latter part of his business life he had some reverses. During this temporary period I asked him if he ever thought about the many millions he had given away, now that he was not as wealthy. He replied, "Of course I have, but remember, I never lost a dollar of the money I gave. I only lost what I kept."

Priority for Spending

A hundred and twenty-five young business and professional people asked me to lead a Saturday seminar on personal finance. They understood little about spending by priority. Together we worked out five steps which have proven helpful to them:

1. *Define the necessities*—This takes more than making a list; it requires definition of the items on the list. For example, transportation is a necessity, but a new automobile is not. Decent clothes are needed, but they don't have to come from Brooks Brothers or Bonwit Teller. Food is an essential, but eating out in fancy restaurants is not. Once a Jewish friend who had lived through a concentration camp experience was talking about defining necessities. I suggested that many of us could live on much less than we do, and he very poignantly said, "You have no idea how little." The first priority is necessities.

2. *Personal development*—Part of everything we make should be earmarked for personal development, yet we get just as much good out of reading a book from the library as one we buy, though it is not as convenient. A tour of the local museum is often as beneficial as a visit to one in a far city. Often local colleges provide excellent evening opportunities very reasonably.

3. *Savings*—Savings are a decision, a discipline. They are never a pleasure. There is never enough money left over for savings. Savings have to be budgeted.

4. *Good memories*—In every period of our life we need some good memories to look back on, and they cost money. They don't have to be terribly expensive, but a certain amount of money should be spent creating good memories in each unique period of our life so we can look back with pleasure. Our son and his wife married on very little money and on their honeymoon went to an expensive French restaurant in New Orleans. It was an elegant evening. When he told me about it he wondered if I might question his wisdom, but I didn't; he was buying a good memory. It would be foolish to go often, but a great night on a great occasion is an investment in good memories, and memories pay lifetime dividends.

5. *Spend to impress others*—It may surprise you that we put this in the list, but I felt fortunate in getting the group to put it fifth instead of first. So often, much of our spending is to impress our neighbors and families or associates with our prosperity. It's easy to convince the foolish that one must "spend money to make money," or "look prosperous and become prosperous." The group simply recognized all of us are going to waste some to impress others; therefore, we put it last hoping it would not affect the major part of our budget or derail it totally by being first.

Post-Note

I close my thoughts on money, hoping that they have been helpful, by paying tribute to our free enterprise system. But I must also say that I do not believe the system alone has produced the American standard of living with its abundance of options. I believe the unique combination of the Puritan ethic and freedom was the marriage that gave birth to our high standard of living. The Puritanical sense of responsibility, belief in hard work and conviction that every man has a talent and will stand one day before God and be judged for the use of that talent, was permitted to grow in an environment of freedom for the first time in history. Our extremely high-option life evolved as the fruit of this union.

With very little understanding for this combination of responsibility and freedom, we now go over the world insisting on freedom for people who have little sense of responsibility. Freedom is not our best export. Our best export is a "sense of responsibility." By exporting freedom, alone, we are giving a formula for frustration. Freedom is a means, never an end in itself. Only the responsible will bless the world in their freedom.

Some historians have said the danger of the Puritan ethic is that it makes people conscious of their responsibility to work and utilize their God-given talents which in turn creates wealth. The production of this wealth, particularly the passing on of wealth, creates options which the heirs do not have the character to exercise correctly. And so, within a series of generations there is a return to poverty. Certainly one of the oldest sayings is, "From shirtsleeves to shirtsleeves in three generations."

It's unfortunate that we cannot develop character as easily as we can develop wealth. We are fortunate when they grow together. Those with the character to make proper decisions on the options money brings become mature enough to handle any amount of money. I sincerely hope responsibility and opportunity are yours.

THINK ABOUT IT . . .

It is better to be esteemed, respected, than applauded.

Intelligent individuals use their circumstances as their discipline.

It is better to share the silence of wise men than the conversation of fools.

Some people travel, others wander, and still others, unfortunately, simply escape.

Opportunity is always unlimited—it's our talent, motivation, and dedication that are limited.

Hard work is the slag that must be refined to get luck.

Ignorance, like poverty, doesn't take much effort.

As soon as you learn to take yourself completely seriously, you have great possibilities of becoming a total fool.

The danger of guilt is that it will make us accept a lowered evaluation of ourselves.

William James said, "The first step in changing any behavior is to start immediately."

You can be sure that the man who brags about his humble beginnings has moved a long way from his starting place.

One's early success is generally bought with leisure time.

On the isle of Bali, they have a saying, "Our highest art is the way we live each day."

It takes a con man to ask others to respect him when he doesn't respect himself.

Some folks pray to God for money because they think He is more sympathetic than the local banker.

I am only fully invested when I've invested myself.

You can repay a loan but never a favor.

The Lord has given you the power to get wealth, but He has not given you the wealth.

Many reach out their hands for material things because their minds are too small to hold ideas.

Once wealthy individuals were called "men of means" and that was a good concept regarding wealth.

Unfortunately, in today's world it seems a profit is without honor.

You know you have become a true giver when you get as excited about a giving opportunity as you do about a good investment opportunity.

Debt is the only financial discipline the indulgent will accept.

Pr 30.8, 9

2

YOUR HEROES

Someone to Look Up To

We cannot live fully without heroes, for they are the stars to guide us upward. They are the peaks on our human mountains. Not only do they personify what we can be, but they also urge us to be. Heroes are who we can become if we diligently pursue our ideals in the furnace of our opportunities.

Heroes are those who have changed history for the better. They are not always the men and women of highest potential, but those who have exploited their potential in society's behalf. Their deeds are done not for the honor but for the duty. Through our study of heroes we enter the realities of greatness.

Heroes are the personification of our ideals, the embodiment of our highest values. A society writes its diary by naming its heroes. We as individuals do the same. When Socrates said, "Talk, young man, that I might know you," he could have also added, "Talk of your heroes that I might know not only who you are, but who you will become."

A discerning investor was having lunch with a young man who had recently been made CEO of a corporation. Early in the conversation he asked the young executive to talk of his heroes. The young man named a ruthless military genius and an arrogant executive. From then on, the conversation took a cool turn and ended much sooner than expected. Later, the investor said, "What a shame to turn over an organization to such immaturity." And because of his impression of the young man, he sold his large block of stock, which proved a good decision.

In much the same area, Dr. J. C. Cain of the Mayo Clinic, when selecting the young medical men to be trained at Mayo, had difficulty because of the exceptionally high caliber of all the applicants. All had excellent grades, fine discipline, high motivation, and good work habits. In searching for some question which would differentiate between them, he chose the same process as the investor, "Young man, tell me of your heroes." Dr. Cain found this was the best clue to their value structure.

Those who have no heroes have not yet identified their highest ideals. Greatness demands an appreciation of greatness shown in others. As a person changes his heroes, so he changes the direction of his life. The most unfortunate are those who egotistically become their own heroes, which is as disastrous as becoming one's own god.

Seldom do the pseudosophisticates have heroes and, as Hemingway pointed out, ("As you get older, it is harder to have heroes but it is sort of necessary—some have faded, others have died.") Those who have faded generally fade because our value structure has changed. We are out of phase with who they were. Their value is in holding us to our value structure.

In the '60s we went through an antihero period in which we were deifying the common man. This concept of the common man is a product of rebellion and nothingness in which there is no nobility to stir the spirit nor galvanize the will. Many were trying to see who could be the sloppiest, the slobbiest, and the funkiest. They have chosen the easiest—though not most profitable—way, for the gravity of man's apathy and his trend downward is working in their behalf. Envy and apathy make it easy to be antihero.

Currently the media are demythologizing heroes. Men unwilling to climb to great heights themselves often create slides for those who have climbed above them. Making all men equal, they make all common. The common man has done very little other than to pass life from one generation to the other, awaiting the uncommon man. George Bernard Shaw talks about this in his prologue to *Man and Superman*. Here he describes the common man as the wire that passes the current and the uncommon man as the appliance of life who does the great works. Heroes justify the elitism of responsibility and accomplishment which raise the base on which the common man stands.

Every age needs to add its heroes to the long list, establishing the tradition of values. As Shakespeare said, "So shall inferior eyes that borrow their behaviors from the great, grow great by your example and put on the dauntless spirit of resolution." Heroes not only inspire us, but they prove the greatness of which the human spirit is capable. In looking up, we are drawn up.

Generally, heroes cannot be current, for as Will Rogers said, "Being a hero is about the shortest-lived profession on earth." Generations must pass before history's spotlight is able to correctly shine on those who are to be our heroes. Rudyard Kipling put it this way, "It is the next generation that, looking over its own, will see the heroes of our own time clearly." We cannot be so anxious to be living among heroes that we try to identify them. Better to use the current ones as models and let history select them as heroes.

As illustrations rather than recommendation, I will name specific men who I believe have heroic qualities: such men as the apostle Paul, Leonardo da Vinci, Albert Einstein, Mahatma Gandhi, Abraham Lincoln, Anwar Sadat. Though only a partial list, these will suffice to help in identifying personal heroes. I have chosen each for an outstanding trait of character which, in emulation, would enoble my own life.

The apostle Paul was total dedication personified. He had gone through what Oswald Chambers called his "white funeral," in which he had literally died to himself; his "black funeral," being the physical death, would come later. He was one of the few men whom I feel that I personally know just from having studied him. He could say, with assurance, "This one thing I do." He had made up his mind. He had found his magnificent obsession, his lodestar, the race that he was to run.

Gandhi personifies dedicated unselfishness. He found a love for his people who deserved justice. He had in him that spark of greatness which was ignited when he was thrown off the train in a racial incident. Often such an incident galvanizes a person. Similarly, I knew of a labor leader who became internationally known after management had foolishly watered him down with a hose in subzero weather. Such events galvanize men of character.

Gandhi personifies our great, though subconscious, desire to sacrifice and be subservient to something bigger than we are, particularly when we feel that we personally can influence it. Part of the great frustration of the nuclear situation is that so many people feel the impending doom but feel totally helpless to do anything about it. Gandhi didn't settle for walking around the streets with a picket sign. He personified the answer. As one of my heroes, he embodies the values which I feel are the answers to life, not just the questions. He had the will to stand and be counted, though he sacrificed his life doing it.

In our times, *Anwar Sadat* personified the largeness of character, the nobility of spirit, the willingness to forgive and to risk his life doing it. His magnanimous spirit made him a giant among us. When he came to power, few expected him to rise to any such heights, because they did not know the bigness of his spirit. Sadat rose to the situation much as Harry Truman did, and he will go down in history for that trait which our heroes show and for which we secretly yearn: bigness of spirit.

Abraham Lincoln combined strength and gentleness. He could do his duty as he saw it though it tore his heart in two as he did it. He didn't seem to possess a superior gift but a superior spirit that matched the opportunity. He was able to be flexible without changing course or values. He lacked personal happiness but he had abiding joy.

Albert Einstein would probably be selected by few people as a hero, largely because he was revered for a gift of intelligence beyond what we find available to most of us. We seldom make a hero out of those who are so far above us that we cannot identify with them. Einstein is one of my personal heroes, not for his intellect but for his humility. I love to look in his simple, childlike eyes and see the wonder and awe that he obviously felt for life, the universe, and God. His humility was a natural state, not an acquired or disciplined accomplishment. Just as true confidence is the absence of cockiness or fear, so his humility was the absence of arrogance rather than the presence of some specific quality we call humility. His humility seemed to accrete. It was the humility that often becomes the natural state of the truly great. Einstein seemed devoid of arrogance, self-centeredness, and conceit—for these ignoble traits had been replaced by a mental and spiritual temper which let him see his ignorance much more than his knowledge—and his gratitude far beyond his rights.

Leonardo da Vinci saw life whole and was relaxed to let it be. He didn't mount a campaign to change anything, for he, probably more than any other man, understood more fully the great unifying principles of life. Science, art, music, mathematics, or philosophy—they were all the same, and man was the unifying principle of creation. He never attempted to author or manipulate truth, just to understand it. He was on the exciting "journey of the mind" and grateful for the trip. He left so little in the way of completed accomplishment that the historian Hart, though he recognized his intellect ("probably the greatest intellect that any man has ever had"), did not list him among those hundred selected as the great accomplishers of all ages. Because da Vinci understood principles, his mind could range indefinitely, creating sketchy ideas of such great magnitude that it would take hundreds of years before they were brought to useful adaptation. He understood that life was bigger than himself, so he relaxed and enjoyed it—not by loafing but by thinking. Some called him lazy, but he felt "the more the genius, the less the work." I feel he had a very deep, real reverence for God, similar to Einstein. To me, he is an intellectual hero and his serenity a personal reproach to our hurry, scurry, activist culture. It's nice and comfortable to realize we are only a small dot in a very big picture—God's eternal universe.

Abraham is a biblical hero of vision and faith. He was willing to risk all on the unseen, the transcendental, for he knew the soft facts of life ultimately overcome the hard facts of science. He ventured into a relationship which became his reality. We need heroes to personify vision, for without vision we settle on too low a plateau.

Furthermore, I need heroes to personify persistence. In a very practical way, *Edison* does this as well as anyone, for any man who can fail three hundred times and take the attitude, "Fortunately for us we now know three hundred of the wrong ways, which means we are gaining on the right way," is a hero of persistence. Kipling said it well, "If you can see the things you've given your life to torn down by knaves and build them back with worn-out tools . . . you'll be a man, my son." There are times in all our lives when we need someone to personify the will to survive, the refusal to give up. Coach Tom Landry told me quarterback Roger Staubach contributed this belief to football: "You can win in the last two minutes." That is a fine legacy to leave to the game.

It is not conventional to choose a hero from your hobby. However, I have great respect and need for consistency, and golfer *Ben Hogan* is the personification of consistency.

He paid the price; and while he is recognized for his tenacity and coming back after an accident and overcoming handicaps, the thing I admire about him is the fact that he was willing to consistently study the golf swing until he could make it repeatable, which is the secret of good golf.

The list could go on and on, naming the great of the past to whom we could look, with profit, as heroes personifying those traits of character and value which we would like to make part of our own. For example, every Southerner has to think of *Robert E. Lee* as an illustration of a magnanimous man. And the same is true of *Booker T. Washington,* who accomplished great things in the face of obstacles others could not overcome. The noble is ultimately the practical.

We are unrealistic to think our heroes should be perfect, for then, when we discover their weaknesses, they topple from their rightly deserved pedestals. Does it really matter that our heroes are less than perfect? Why should a few faults cause us to minimize their true greatness?

The Bible recognizes that heroes are not perfect. One of the proofs of the inspiration of Scripture is that the Bible says things about its characters that people would not write. In the hall of faith, found in Hebrews, we see people like Rahab mentioned and described as a prostitute—but still she is in the hall of faith. The list includes murderers, schemers, adulterers.

The media and the book-trade prostitutes have done the nonthinking a great disservice in getting them to exchange the lasting inspiration of the hero for the momentary excitement of the celebrity. Our son first caused me to think about the difference between heroes and celebrities when he said, "The heroes of the early church were martyrs and ours are celebrities." Herein may lie a great deal of the weakness of our church. Not that we should foster martyrdom, for there's no one more hypocritical than a self-professed martyr looking to be sacrificed. Yet persecution has always been known as the greatest purifying agent of religion. Emerson said, "Those who follow after celebrity sip the foam of many lives." Our celebrities rise on a wave of applause and break on the rocks of inattention. They are fantasy waiting to be exposed.

There is no need to defend our heroes against anything except perfection. When we ask for perfection in heroes, we become vulnerable to those who expose our heroes' weaknesses and thereby try to destroy their value. Heroes personify the value and the human capability of reaching nobility, but not perfection.

When we demand perfection we are not only unrealistic, we rule out the great who have made mistakes and who have weaknesses of their own—for all of us have weaknesses. Some just have not had the occasion to have theirs exposed or tested. Humankind is not able to accomplish perfection, so we must not be disillusioned and give up on our heroes simply because they are not perfect. To expect perfection is to build on a false philosophical, even theological, base.

Heroes Share at Least Four Qualities

1. *They are real*—not myth or fantasy. A young black who had been a "holy terror" became a Christian. He told his sister he was going to become a preacher. She said, "Be real, man, be real." There is no way for a hero to be a phony in the area of his heroism. The man raising the flag on Iwo Jima may have died a hopeless drunk, but he was real when he raised that flag. Heroes are not gods nor demigods; they are real people—not perfect, but real.

2. *Dedication*—heroes live with a purpose and many die for a cause. They faced a situation that became bigger than themselves, something they were willing to give themselves to. They found and responded to a situation which most of us feel deep inside—the haunting desire to give

ourselves to something bigger than we are. Yet few heroes sought that situation, but when it came they were capable of a dedication totally beyond themselves.

3. *Concentration*—while dedication precedes and fosters concentration, it does not automatically accomplish it. Concentration is the ability to think of the right thing at the right time. It requires poise in the face of opposition, mental discipline amid confusion, the kind of resolution and persistence that caused the apostle Paul to say, "This one thing I do."

4. *Sacrifice*—in a great sense they lived their life or sacrificed their time, talent, possessions—or even life—for those of us who look up to them. They have been remembered, not for what they got, but for what they gave. They were the responsible ones. Many had the opportunity to choose a lower road, but their sense of responsibility made them choose the higher road. They sacrificed their standard of living for their standard of giving. The "me generation" through which we passed did not have the attitude of heroes.

In selecting heroes to emulate, or even to idealize, we should look more at their traits of character than at their accomplishments. Accomplishments are proportional to opportunity. Societies have numerically weighted their hero worship in favor of military figures—not necessarily because society desires to be military, but because war challenges the best that is within man. As Hemingway said, the only noble sports are those in which a man risks his life, such as bullfighting, automobile racing, and mountain climbing. These require the courage, the concentration, and the willingness to risk the ultimate of life which becomes life itself.

We might justify our military heroes as being the protectors of our society, because they have saved us in military situations. However, subconsciously I believe it is their personification of the traits of nobility which we all wish for but either have not the occasion or the capacity to attain. A hero is someone who is all that a person should be under the demands of the occasion.

While our American philosophy, based on our Judeo-Christian theology, has been one of hero recognition, the Bible has been very instructive to us by its surprising revelation of the heroes of the faith and their weaknesses: Abraham lied; Jacob was sneaky; David was moody, immoral, and a murderer; Jonah was a traitor and a coward; Joseph was arrogant with his brothers; Peter was a denier and a coward; Paul was a persecutor. They all knew their sins and imperfections—but they refused to let their weakness keep them from using their strength which made them do acts of heroism and become the stalwarts we call heroes.

An important lesson in studying heroes is that often somewhere in their life they had a desert period, often of public rejection, and came back like the phoenix, having stood for a cause worth standing for.

Some of the Lessons We Learn from Heroes

1. We must be men and women for our times. From the conditions of our time we derive our strength and our defects. Thomas Carlyle said, "Society is founded on hero worship." History is the story of the effect of great men and women. They shaped their times for good.

2. Occasionally we need to stop saying great things about our heroes and ask ourselves what they would say about us. Our heroes can become the verbs in our lives.

3. Heroes must survive for a long time as examples of trustworthy values, in season and out. The apostle Paul deserves hero status. I know of very few men who have named Nero as their hero. Today we name our children Paul and call our dogs Nero. It's not being a winner today that may count tomorrow.

4. We should know how to make ourselves feel small by comparison with heroes. By compressing ourselves in this positive, healthy way, we know more the essence of

ourselves in relation to the values we inherit from our heroes. It is this discipline that always inspires and makes room for growth.

> Lives of great men all remind us,
> we can make our lives sublime.
> And, departing, leave behind us
> footprints on the sands of time.

Our daughter Brenda knew how I enjoyed these four lines. On my study wall is a framed plaque with sand glued to a board. On that she pasted a footprint of each of her three children, made when they were very small. In her quiet, persuasive way, she was reminding me that my grandchildren's footsteps are walking somewhat behind my own. Heroes don't have to be famous; they only have to be heroic. Who are yours?

THINK ABOUT IT . . .

Few heroes ever started out to be that. Those who did generally ended up as clowns.

We choose our heroes as illustrations of our highest values.

Heroes are the guiding stars in our earthly firmament.

While celebrities may dazzle us, heroes enlarge us.

A great man sees his talent as a responsibility, while others see it as luck or favor.

Our models die but our heroes never do.

Most people have a passion for significance.

3

YOUR MODELS

Choose Them Carefully

While our heroes inspire us to *be,* our models help us to *do.* *Role Model* is a good current term, for our role is our function—not who we are, but what we do. Our models are to help us achieve the best use of our talents. They show us how to be useful, how to link our passion to our activity.

Therefore, our philosophy of function is important. I firmly believe every normal person has been given at least one talent and many have received multiple talents. We are responsible for the use we make of that talent. We function most successfully when we are utilizing what we can do best, rather than what we wish we could do. Fortunate individuals learn early in life to say to themselves and mean it, "I have been given a talent; therefore I am responsible for using it for 'the common good' of my society and, [if Christian], for the glory of God." What is *your* greatest, dominant talent?

Service is the rent we pay for our space in life. The better the space, the higher the rent. Those of us who live in the high-rent section should not complain about the extra service expected of us. This is not only scriptural but common wisdom: "To whom much has been given,

80

much is required." No one inherits life-space rent-free. Poachers on life's territory eventually become dispossessed and exposed for the frauds they are. If in economics there are no "free lunches," certainly in life there is no free space. If you aren't paying your rent, someone else is. It is our moral obligation to contribute. As Thomas à Kempis said, "He cannot continue long at peace who does not strive to be the servant of all."

Listen to men of great accomplishment and you repeatedly hear them refer to their models—the teacher who made learning exciting, the boss who made work meaningful, or the parent who made life whole. Once spending a few hours privately with Billy Graham, I remarked about his graciousness, which I had observed since his early twenties. He quickly responded, "Whatever I have, I inherited from my father who was such a gracious man."

Heroes we idolize and models we emulate. Models differ from heroes, as principles differ from techniques. In models we personify desirable traits, functions, and techniques. Generally they are more current than heroes, and a personal relationship with a model is preferable. A person is easier to emulate than an essay. We are able to query our models and share in the dynamism that drives them. We borrow from their motivation.

From the young we are continually hearing the catchy phrase, "Accept me for myself alone"—what narcistic tommyrot! Can you imagine a football coach hearing a talented but debauched player saying, "Coach, accept me as I am. Leave me on the team even though I'm too tired to play today. I will just sit here and cheer when the others do well. I'll even drink water and leave the Gatorade for those who are sweating"? His nobility of attitude notwithstanding will get him kicked off the team because he is not fulfilling his function. He wasn't put on the team to cheer— he was put there to play. Depriving himself of the Gatorade doesn't make up for the fact that he is not sweating for the common good.

The secret of modeling is that we build the reality of the quality into our lives rather than merely imitating techniques. Like Epictetus said, "Imagine for yourself a character, a model personality whose example you determine to follow in private as well as in public." Imitation does not make us the functioning person we want to be, while emulation will. Robert Louis Stevenson was one of our great literary figures because he became the traits which he saw in others. For example, he said, "I have thus played the sedulous ape to Hazlitt, to Lamb, to Wordsworth, to Sir Thomas Browne, to DeFoe, to Hawthorne, to Montaigne, to Baudelaire, and to Obermann." These were his to emulate, not to merely imitate.

The brilliant Dr. Shervert Frazier, whom I knew as a young man and who has now gone on to become an internationally known psychiatrist, once said to me, "I can very nearly predict a person's behavior if I know how a boy defines a man and a girl defines a woman." While we rarely find an individual who totally defines either a man or woman, we collect as we go along traits which we think go into making this composite, and we personify them. Growing up in the poor, earthy—even primitive—part of a large city, I saw the male qualities involved in survival. It was either the strongest, toughest, meanest, two-fistedest kid on the block or the cleverest who did the best. Eventually the clever ones organized the physical ones. As we grow older, it takes years to sort out this type of role modeling to see what it is we really want in our lives. I make the point that possibly we never really do an adequate job until we very consciously decide the traits, functions, and skills which we want and choose our models accordingly.

While a personal relationship with models is preferable, it is not always possible. So we often turn to literary figures, for they have exerted tremendous power over many of our high achievers. Ray Stedman modeled his Scripture teaching after G. Campbell Morgan, whom he never met.

In a novel he was reading, Chaim Potok became friends of an imaginary English family. The characters became so real to him, they eventually led him into being one of our great men of letters, though it caused Potok to be removed from the Hasidic rabbinate.

Once we have gone through the discipline of selecting in others the traits of personality—character, intelligence, functions, and skills—which we want to personify, we can start the search for the models. If I did not use this process, I would not be writing about it. I have followed it and I recommend it.

Let me tell you an experience which was helpful to me as a young man. As a youth I read *Think and Grow Rich*, which helped me not the least bit in making money—but it had a thought concerning "a personal board of directors" which I adapted to develop certain characteristics within myself. I picked out eight qualities for my life which I saw personified in various men I knew. I asked them for an autographed picture which I framed and placed in a circle which I could see every day. It sounds corny now, but knowing how deeply I felt about this, I probably would do it again. I also framed the Hoffman's head of Christ and put it at the head of the circle and framed a plain mirror, putting it at the bottom where I could look at myself and then look at these others and consider my growth in the particular qualities which I felt were needed in my life. Benjamin Franklin did something similar when he listed thirteen qualities each on separate cards, and rotated them, carrying each one with him for a period of time.

The important thing is not the qualities that someone else has selected but the system of selecting and the discipline of following through on the development that is important to you. Often people ask me what the qualities were and I won't tell. They were strictly personal and by telling them I'd be broadcasting my own self-analysis, which is not what I'm trying to do.

I preferred to select my role models from among individuals I knew, agreeing with Thoreau when he said, "Men will believe what they see." The missionary E. Stanley Jones emphasized this when he pointed out that the uniqueness of Christianity was "the Word became flesh," then continued by saying that in other religions "the word remained the word." Precepts are valuable, but in modeling I preferred to personify if possible.

Role models don't have to be famous. Most of them won't be. For example, a photographer, writing about cowboys, said, "I mean really look at them and what they're all about. They're about integrity and dignity and freedom and the best things that people are all about. Not that all cowboys are wonderful, but there's a lot more good in them than in most of us." As long as he saw some trait he wanted to emulate in the cowboy, he had a good model.

That brings us to three traits a model must have for us. First, he must have one of the same talents which we have, for unless we have a common talent, we cannot develop what we are seeing. Next, he has to be better than we currently are. It is generally better to pick out someone who is not superlative but, who is a reasonable distance ahead of us. Thus we will not be inundated by our imperfection but be encouraged by our accomplishment. Then, he or she must be available for observation. It doesn't do much good to see a person once and try to use him or her as a model. The more intimately we can see what our model does and how he does it, the better it is. We need time with the person, if possible, because it takes repeated exposures to form certain traits in our own lives. For example, Jackie Burke, who won fifteen golf tour victories, said, "Watching the good players in Texas was a terrific help—Jimmy Demaret, Byron Nelson, Ben Hogan, Lloyd Mangrum, Ralph Goodall. When you had players like that for models, you had something to shoot at."

Our self-image is important for we must see in our model

what we can become—not what we would like to become
or what we fear to become.

John Stein, the famous restauranteur, invited me to
lunch following an early telecast and we talked of model
stage personalities. He said the first quality of the truly
great is they are able, even from the platform, to establish
that they are a person more than an entertainer. I have
told salesmen that this is also the common denominator
of great salesmen. They come in a selling function and
they leave a personality who happens to be selling. Mr.
Stein said that in his experience only the relaxed have
the capability for longevity. The frantic soon burn out.

Some "losers" by popular standards are still excellent
models even though America is a society that "worships
the winner." Losing is thought stupid; it is considered almost antisocial. Whatever the reason for losing, it is never
justified. Even in Christian circles this philosophy has permeated on the very spurious basis that "God don't make
no flops." However, it is hard to see Calvary as a winner's
coronation or a meeting of celebrities. Once I was asked
by a highly successful executive to name someone whom
I felt could give a good testimony on giving and philan-
thropy. Since Maxey Jarman had given millions of dollars,
I suggested him. But I was reminded that due to the problems he was having in the corporation, he had "lost his
credibility," meaning he was not currently considered a
winner. In a society that chooses celebrities over martyrs,
we can expect harsh treatment for losers. However, many
losers in their very being personify some of our best traits.
I am reminded of what Abraham Lincoln said, "I'd rather
lose in a cause that will ultimately succeed than succeed
in one that will ultimately fail."

I have found great stimulation in watching the physically
handicapped overcome their disability. I might not agree
with George Wallace's politics, but I agree with his determination to become governor for the fourth time in Alabama from a wheelchair. To see Franklin Roosevelt walking

on the arm of his son with dignity said to every handicapped person, "It can be done." Only those of us who have lived with a physical handicap of some kind know the constant irritation and the need to see recurring cases of individuals who have conquered their disability. Nothing stirs my corpuscles like the story of someone winning by the rules against the odds.

Often we are able to use athletes as models because athletic contests are really a metaphor for life. Coach Tom Landry is a model to me of discipline. The "Hail Mary" pass by Roger Staubach has become part of the football vocabulary.

Often athletes adopt even the mannerisms of their models. For example, many of the running backs are like instant replays of Jimmy Brown's greatness, not by running as effectively as he, but by getting up slowly as if hurt and creeping back into the huddle just in time to explode again. Often the slow play on a golf course is because duffers have watched professionals on tour read the greens. They sight the pendulum, hitch up their pants with their thumbs, freeze over a putt like Jack Nicklaus, yip like Ben Hogan, and miss "the same old way." They find it much easier to model the equipment and the mannerisms than the discipline and the talent.

The behavioralists make a strong case for our environment and the effect of role models in molding us. I cannot accept that we are completely a product of our environment so long as we have a will which can greatly modify our environment. Children from the same family turn out differently, just as individuals in a neighborhood will go in different directions. Dr. Haddon Robinson, who was a white child in the slums of black Harlem, has gone on to be president of the Conservative Seminary in Denver. He had to exercise his will and select his models differently from those who chose to stay or even to move on to penal institutions. The will is crucial.

The courage Kipling wrote into his "If" is the courage of maturity:

If you can meet with triumph and disaster
And treat those two impostors just the same,

Genuine courage is rare. As Eric Hoffer explains, "Doubting our self-worth we are terrified of independent thinking; therefore, we prefer to be agents of a larger cause or vision. By these belief systems we are told how to act and what to believe. They lend nobility and meaning to our lives." Individuals are like light bulbs seeking a socket, which we identify as a cause. The doctrine of the group becomes our electric current.

We need to personify the wisdom of courage. Too often we take confrontation as a duty in which we start a fight, not as a responsibility in which morally we have no alternative but to stand. I sometimes feel that our fear of failing to stand causes us to impulsively start the confrontation before we lose our nerve.

We need models in such mundane things as skills—particularly the philosophy toward skill. At eighty, the best bootmaker in the world is Dunn of Texas. In an interview he was telling about a young man who came to him and asked him how long it would take to become a good bootmaker. Dunn said, "I can't tell you, because I don't know how long you're going to live, but it will take your whole life." He emphasized that every boot should be better than the last one. His answer brings to memory the thrilling "Chambered Nautilus" of Oliver Wendell Holmes:

> Build thee more stately mansions, O my soul,
>   As the swift seasons roll!
>   Leave thy low-vaulted past!
> Let each new temple, nobler than the last,
> Shut thee from heaven with a dome more vast,
>   Till thou at length art free,
> Leaving thine outgrown shell by life's unresting sea!

In a non-self-directed society, where values and directions are picked up from the current milieu, it is important to avoid false "role models." Advertising recognizes the power of celebrities on ordinary people. They tell us that we are able vicariously to enjoy what they enjoy, just so long as we buy or use what they use. The sensible question, "What possible connection is there between what they are doing and what I am doing?", seems to be totally lost in the euphoria and fantasy of advertising.

Entertainers and athletes have automatic entry into the world of the young. Dope and sex rode in on the lyrics of the music. The young in turn paid amazing financial and popular tribute to those entertainers. Probably I am among the few who believe that many of these celebrities would not appeal individually to young people at all. En masse on television and at rock concerts, however, they are able to inundate perfectly sensible, normal kids with the fantasy, appealing to the very baseness of our nature.

Lest we feel smug, adults have not been in the least immune to this. I've seen executives enamored of men who made huge fortunes in highly creative, though ethically questionable, ways. As long as the man made megabucks, he was admired, accepted, and only criticized when his Midas magic began to fail.

I think most serious people are concerned that we are in a period in history where mediocrity is the model. One of the things that disturbs me most about the absorbing motion picture, The Verdict, was the fact that the leading character came on the stage as a drunk and left it the same way. He was shown to be the weak victim of the establishment, and his crowning achievement was beating the establishment in one legal case. I felt the strong audience reaction was that a man who started out second in his class could end up a mediocre ambulance-chaser and still come back to beat the system one time, gloriously. I fail to see this as an inspiring model, particularly when fortuitous circumstances had played such a big part in his victory.

We dare not choose models who have great accomplishments only once, such as the lawyer in *The Verdict.* To go from underdog to topdog is thrilling, and if there are consistent reasons, such people are worth modeling, but we can't depend on fortuitous circumstances. There is no way to model a lucky person.

While we do not choose to be around negative models, in the course of life we are thrown with people who become this to us. I once had a sales manager whom I considered my greatest negative model. Whatever he did, I felt that I could do in reverse and be assured of being right for me. He was like a left-handed carpenter trying to drive a bent nail into a mahogany log with a banana. Because my experience with him was negatively positive, I have said to many young people, "If you have a choice, always work for either the best or the worst boss, for from the good ones you learn what to do and from the bad ones you learn what not to do. From those who are mediocre, you learn practically nothing."

As we develop and mature, we often find the need to change models. Just as we outgrow our need for certain books, we outgrow our need for certain models and need to move on to someone whose desirable trait is on a higher level. We do this with teachers, moving from those who teach us the rudiments to those who teach us the esoteric. Nowhere is this more clearly seen than in the arts and music.

Not only do we need to change models when we mature, we also find in our self-examination that we have chosen some bad models. A man who became nationally famous for having had a remarkable turnaround in his life kept clinging to one of his models in his former life, much to his disaster. Often he would suggest that I should meet this notorious man. I had no desire to meet him, any more than I would want to meet Adolf Hitler or Mao Tse-tung. He was a known criminal. Yet my friend continued to hold him in the highest esteem and for what I believe to be the wrong reasons. The man was clever; he had nerve and notoriety. I don't believe that my friend ever became what he could have become if he had turned loose of this early model.

On the other hand, I had a friend who was endowed with an amazingly clever mind. He loved subtlety and complicated machinations. The simple truth was not intriguing enough. He had a mentality that would have made him superior to almost any man with whom he dealt. Still he wanted to deal in a way that was pleasing to him—not just to win, but to win by intrigue. As his spiritual nature developed he saw this as wrong and began to change. This meant dropping some of his earlier clever models and coming to a more direct way of dealing with truth.

I personally believe that he has averted a real danger in his life which a former associate of mine failed to correct. He was, likewise, a very clever though uneducated man. He had an amazing ability with figures and could work complicated mathematical structures in his mind faster than others could have done with a calculator. For example, in business he would give someone a proposition and then a second and a third, making them feel that the third was better than the first when it was not. His cleverness with figures became so intriguing to him that he kept going farther and farther away from honesty until eventually he broke the law. He was one of my early models whom I had to discard. While I've kept many of the fine early lessons I learned from him, I saw him becoming clever for cleverness' sake.

Dr. Richard Halverson, Chaplain of the United States Senate, also faced a model change. He tells how his attitude toward the church was first established by an irreverent relative and how it remained that way until he met a young minister who not only changed his attitude, but created within him the desire to become a minister.

While we are choosing our models, we must accept the fact that others may be choosing us. One night I was crossing the Baylor University campus after lecturing, when a young man walked up and put his arm on my shoulder and said, "You do not know me, but today during your lecture I saw who I wanted to be." It startled me, for I was not totally sure what he meant. But if he had chosen me as one of his models, I pray he saw a strength, not a weakness.

It's important how we picture ourselves as role models. I have found that one of the most exasperating truths of being a father is that my children picked up the things I genuinely model much more readily than the preachments which I gave. We have to remember someone is watching and it isn't Big Brother; it is little brother, or Jack, or the warehouseman. Once I was coming out of the plant when the night watchman said to me, "Mr. Smith, I sure wish I had your income, but I sho' don't want your worry." I realized that he saw my job in my face as worry, while I thought about it as responsibility. I needed to brighten up my face.

A most intriguing study would be to follow the chain of modeling, seeing how one person has influenced another through generations. For example, C. S. Lewis was greatly influenced by both Chesterton and George Mac-Donald. Lewis, in turn, has influenced Chuck Colson who today is influencing our entire prison system.

When we think about our responsibility as a model, we should remember what the apostle Paul said, "Follow me as I follow Christ."

Summary

Our selection and use of models is largely controlled by our self-image. We cannot become what we cannot see ourselves becoming. As we see ourselves, so we draw to ourselves those aids which develop us. Therefore, it is important for us to see in our models the person we can and truly want to become.

THINK ABOUT IT . . .

Peculiarities in a great man will not weaken him but indiscretions will.

Models show us how to be useful.

The superior man has a fertile mind, a deep understanding, a cultivated taste. And a disciplined life.

People are not driven into perfection by rules but, rather, drawn in by example.

You should see in your model what you ultimately want to be.

"To live for a time close to great minds is the best kind of education." *John Buchan*

4

YOUR MENTORS

They'll Keep You Growing

However far we go in school, the day we graduate is really the day our education begins. For, as Einstein wittily said, "Education is what you learn after you have forgotten everything you learned in school." When we leave school, we leave our prescribed teachers, textbooks, and daily routine, and go on our own—private entrepreneurs in a new world of personal development.

Those who feel they are educated at graduation will slowly turn into disposable dinosaurs, like one engineer whom we eventually let go because graduating from Purdue was the last thing he ever did. After graduating he quit learning, for he thought he had it made. Bobby Nichols explained it neatly in golf terms: "When you think you've got it in this game, that's when you've had it."

Sydney Harris wrote, "Education is not a mass of facts or inert ideas, as Whitehead called them, but an attitude and appetite and approach, a frame of mind, a function of the full personality, of the will, the spirit, and the imagination as much as of the intellectual force."

No one can let up and keep up. A healthy mind is a growing mind. A healthy human is a growing human—mind, spirit, and emotion.

Quality education doesn't have to take place in schools, nor does it have to have a degree to be valid. Some of the most thoroughly educated have attended no institutions of higher learning nor received a degree—but they have drawn from others and thought for themselves—earning a genuine education. On the other hand, those who are proud of being "self-educated" are liable to claim other silly things, like being "self-made." Self-education is anemic education. Truly intelligent people know they have not been self-educated. Who knows enough to educate himself? The truly educated have been mentored, either in person or by reading or association, by superior minds with greater skills and mature spirits.

In mentoring there are two functions—instruction and coaching. Instruction is what Plato referred to as transferring information from one mind to the other. Much of the technological information can be transferred by instructors. Instruction deals with how to do something useful—something for which one has a talent and something one can swap in the market for financial return and recognition as a craftsman. Coaching on the other hand, is the process of developing unique qualities in the art of learning. For example, such things as thinking, feeling, and dedication to excellence cannot be given by instruction—they can only be developed by coaching/mentoring.

Composer Ned Rorem of Curtis Institute said, "Composition cannot be taught. But young composers can learn what to do and how to do it from those who have been through the same processes themselves." I would agree with this and would add that success cannot be taught. But the young can learn what to do and how to do it from those who have been through the same processes themselves. While success can't be taught, it can be caught—however, only by those who hold a vigil for catching it.

Therefore, we need instructors as well as mentors. With an instructor we share an interest in the subject and the ability to communicate with each other on the subject. It is not important whether we like each other or socialize together. Our mutual interest is knowing the subject, not knowing each other.

Mentoring is different. Our best mentors are those with whom we share a common philosophy of life, knowing that what we do is an expression of our philosophy. Personally I have found that I can best be a mentor to those whom I respect most. That respect creates an atmosphere in which they learn the arts of development, since we are not dealing with technique alone. Mentoring involves the heart as well as the head. Our greatest mentors are those who are also our models. This is one of the problems with modern education . . . many teachers want to be instructors only, not willing to accept the responsibility of being models for their students. Our teachers, many of them, were our early models. Girls particularly wanted to be teachers, "like Miss Brown." We remember dedicated teachers who were great human beings from whom we learned how to make a life as well as a living. That modeling many times was more important than the information. As Anna Freud, whose theories advanced the work of her famous father, Sigmund, said, "I didn't go to college, but I had a wonderful father."

The requirements of a good mentor are many. First, (I repeat), we share a compatible philosophy.

Second, the mentor genuinely believes in our potential. Some of the greatest football players have come from tiny schools that receive no publicity, but scouts saw in those players a potential that great coaching could bring out. It is impossible to be serious about a student in whom you really feel there is no great potential. And the student needs to feel the importance of sharing his true potential.

The secret of coaching is to help a person get to where he or she is willing to go. By his superior vision and experience, a coach should be able to let that person see that there are further goals which he or she can reach by discipline. But still the student has to see, believe, and make the effort.

An honest mentor will make an evaluation and sometimes direct the student in another direction—or even to another mentor. My greatest ambition was to sing at the Metropolitan. I did not have the talent but did not know it. The day came when Dr. Charles F. Bryan told me, "Fred, you have everything except talent and, without that, all the practice and discipline and hope will not accomplish what you want to be—so I suggest you find another field." I have never been more depressed, yet deep in my heart I knew he was right. So I completely gave it up and went into business, wherein I discovered a latent talent in myself.

Mediocre people will often display great talent but will not accomplish much because they want to be connected to the coach by association rather than by accomplishment. This is a strange fact, but such people find recognition, even security, in association. They have a fear of trying, failing, and then being thought a loser. High accomplishers stay connected, both to themselves and to their coach, by accomplishment.

The best mentors are always under a mentor. I am afraid of a teacher who isn't also being taught. I distrust gurus, for I don't know who the guru is being "gurued" by. When I hear that top coaches like Tom Landry meet in small groups and help each other, then I understand more how they are able to help others. The highly successful Glenn Baldwin, president of Baldwin Financial Group, has met for years with a small group of financial chief executive officers who swap ideas and suggestions. Growth is never static; it's a constantly changing, dynamic process.

Mentors must be willing to be committed, serious, and available to their students. Nowhere is this more evident than in music. New York Philharmonic Conductor Zubin Mehta, speaking of a young pianist said, "I cannot teach him how to play, for he knows what the composer wanted to say; I can simply help him say it."

Mentors use different systems. I have had two great mentors. One was a philosopher who quietly answered my questions and asked me his. The other was a business executive who had none of the teacher in him. He simply assigned responsibility and reviewed results, but he let me sit in on enough of his activities to see how he worked. Some mentors confront, others challenge or compete. Some congratulate, but some give very faint praise (like the chef who, in four years of apprenticeship, said only one word of praise to a young man who later became a great chef). He said he never forgot the praise, but the lack of it didn't keep him from becoming a great chef because of the helpful attitude of his mentor. He knew his mentor was committed to him, interested in him, and serious about his becoming a great chef. Too much affirmation can be evidence of a lack of deep confidence in the ultimate accomplishment. Praise also can be a cheap cover-up for mediocre mentoring.

Having been mentored for years and having mentored others for quite some time, I make these observations for those being mentored:

1. *Ask your mentor to help you ask the right questions, search in the right places, and stay interested in the right answers.* When we work to know the answers, we find surprising teachers, like the saintly young woman visiting a home for indigent old ladies. She wrote, "The women, like the dozens of homeless folks I have met and now recognize in the streets, are my teachers. They expose my shallow sentimentality, my defense mechanisms, my desire to give easy answers. They nourish my sense of humor, ignite my moral outrage, and draw out my compassion. They often speak in parables. They help me understand why Jesus lived and maybe even why He died. And they ask me, time and again, not to forget those lessons. And not to keep them to myself."

2. *Decide what degree of excellence or perfection you want.* Generally, the object in mentoring is to produce improvement,

not perfection. Only a few can be truly excellent—but all can be better. Begin by being better.

3. *Accept a subordinate, learning position.* Few people can be humble enough to accept concentrated mentoring. They let their ego get in the way and they start to mentor the mentor by trying to impress him with their knowledge or ability. They set up a mental barrier against taking in as fast as he puts out.

4. *Respect the mentor but never idolize him.* Respect lets us accept what he is teaching—but making him an idol removes our critical faculty for fitting his thinking to ourselves.

5. *Put into effect immediately what you are learning.* We seldom are intense about learning anything which we are not going to use very shortly. I was talking to Haddon Robinson, president of Denver Seminary, about giving a personal finance course to the students. He wisely said, "Remember, they will not be intensely interested, because it will be a few years before they will use the material."

In Houston I met a former executive of ours with whom I had lost contact. I found he had a sales-training business. He asked me to monitor his session, and I was amazed at how simple and repetitive it was. I was critical until in the middle of the evening he brought back three or four of the former graduates who had doubled and tripled their sales using his method. He explained that most big sales-training programs give salesmen much more than they can use and so they file the material away in a notebook and continue doing the same things they were doing before they went to the sessions. In his course they learn one thing a night and they go out for the rest of the week and practice that one thing. Then they come back and report the results. The best mentoring is intensity in a narrow field . . . learn, practice, and assimilate.

Once I had the privilege of a lesson in golf from the dean of pros, Harvey Penick. He gave me only one thing to do and then sat and watched quietly while I tried to do it. I had been used to instructors who talked on every shot about many different things to do, but Penick said it once and said nothing else while I was learning to do it. He only watched, and then at the end he gave me the best advice I've ever had in the game: ["May I suggest that you not try to hit any good shots, for you don't have that much talent. Try not to hit any bad ones and you'll be surprised how many people you will beat."]

Mentors understand that they are building unique individuals, not imitators of themselves. A young friend taking up golf asked the pro for help. The pro said, "First, I must know how good you want to be, for if you want to be mediocre I can let you copy me. But if you want to be great, then I've got to spend the time to find out how you can best strike the ball."

Most daily, on-the-job mentoring is nonprofessional, except of course in music and the other arts. But in adult life, the constant mentoring that goes on has no direct financial reward. Therefore, it must have genuine psychic reward. Mentors must feel that they are helping, that they are expanding and extending their contribution to life, that perchance they will participate in somebody's development who will go farther than they were able to in a worthwhile cause.

We not only have a responsibility to *receive* mentoring but to *give* mentoring. When one of my mentors (Maxey Jarman, who built Genesco) died, those who knew our relationship asked me what I was going to do without my "teacher." To which I replied, "I am now old enough and have accumulated enough of his principles that I have a responsibility to pass them on to others." (See next chapter.)

Recently the young vice president of a national organization came to see me, wanting to talk about some of the principles I have written about from time to time. After our visit he wrote and asked me to outline a program for him to follow. I wrote back saying that was his responsibility. And after he finished his program, then I'd be glad to review it with him and make any contribution I could. I wanted to help him go where he wanted to go, not where I wanted him to go—his life was not my responsibility, it was his.

6. *Set up a discipline for relating to the mentor.* Set up an ample and consistent time schedule, select the subject matter in advance. Do your homework to make the sessions profitable.

7. *Reward your mentor with progress and appreciation.* The progress should come first, because if you give him appreciation where there's no progress he knows he has failed. Your progress is his highest reward.

8. *Learn to ask crucial questions*—questions that prove you have been thinking between sessions, questions that show progress in your perception.

9. *Never threaten to give up.* Let him know that you have made a decision for progress, that he is dealing with a persistent person—a determined winner. Then he knows he isn't wasting his time.

Those I have been able to help most are those who have been open to any suggestion or question, not trying to restrict my help to some isolated area when I knew that the root of the matter lay elsewhere. I had a friend who started jogging and found his knees hurting. He went to the doctor who, after examining his knees, asked him to take off his shoes and socks and stand up. My friend was tempted to say, "But Doc, it's my knees that hurt, not my feet." Yet the doctor, out of his medical knowledge, said, "You have flat feet and this is causing your knee trouble." Spiritually, mentally, emotionally, a good mentor is able to see the flat feet that are causing the knees to hurt.

As a practical matter, instructors have to be changed more often than mentors. But mentors themselves need to be surrendered when they have served their function. Seldom is it a personal lifetime commitment to each other—it is a commitment for a purpose. When that purpose is accomplished, the relationship may change to friendship but does not need to be continued as mentor and student. Those mentors who refuse to recognize that they have been used as far as they can go and insist on remaining have lost the real purpose and integrity of their mentoring. They have begun to use the relationship for their own satisfaction and that is ample reason to choose another mentor.

Our needs for mentors change. Sometimes we need teaching much more in the early stages, while we need observing in the later stages. Not only do we want them to observe us technically but to look inside our head and our heart. A Zen Buddhist, teaching life through archery, asked his former students to occasionally send him a picture of themselves drawing a bow so that he might know how they are progressing in their philosophy. (An interesting study for those of you who like the esoteric.)

If you've never watched someone intensely enough to understand how this happens, then you've missed a lot in mentoring. I think Ken Venturi understood this when, telecasting a pro golf tournament in which a young tour professional who had never won before was leading, one of the other commentators said, "That man is going to be a great one, isn't he?" To which Ken replied, "I don't know. He certainly has the physical equipment, but nobody can see inside his heart, and that is where champions differ."

A good mentor can see the hesitation of will, the nervousness of lost poise, the indecision of movement, the tediousness of practice, and the despair of meaninglessness, or the boredom from lack of challenge. These are the difficulties we look to our greatest mentors to solve. For this reason we can help our mentors by being open and real. We cannot play games anymore than we would refuse to take off our clothes for a physical examination. We cannot hide if we are to be helped.

As a mentor, there are certain guidelines I look for in accepting an "apprentice."

1. *The person must have made a commitment to his own development.* And is not looking for me to convince him that he should make a commitment. Alcoholics Anonymous has learned that until that commitment is made, nothing is really possible in development or changing direction. I am a mentor, not an evangelist in career counseling.

2. *People learn slower than we generally expect they should.* Before going into any new business venture I've always followed the rule: "Be prepared to invest 50 percent more money and twice as much time." This prevents panic when progress isn't as fast as I thought it should be. Accomplishment is usually tardy by our preconceived timetable. I have found that people learn, then plateau and assimilate, learn again, plateau and assimilate, learn again, then plateau. Sometimes the plateau time is longer than the climb, or vice versa. Length of time is not important. The quality of continuing progress is—and the attitude of improvement and the dedication to growth.

3. *The results must have meaning.* Viktor Frankl has pointed out in his book, *Man's Search for Meaning,* that the real driving force in life is man's desire for meaning, rather than power, pleasure, or sex. Often these others are simply a road to the destination of meaning. Where a relationship is not accomplishing any real meaningful purpose, it is difficult to maintain any seriousness or dedication to it. I cannot mentor someone in a subject in which I am not deeply involved. Often a mentor's dedication to a subject or an idea is the flame from which the apprentice continually relights his fire.

Dr. Julian Gumperz, who was so meaningful in my life, was studying philosophy. He wanted to specialize in this field. However, he decided that, for his time, economics was more needed than philosophy and that he could not be an honest philosopher when economics was more necessary. So he made economics his emphasis. Thereafter he made his living as an economist but his constant avocation was philosophy. I listened to him with the greatest respect because he was a living philosopher as an economist.

Continually, we who mentor question the mentoring process. For example, can moral virtues and excellence of character always and consistently be taught? No, for every teacher has had his failures. Such failures come when the student does not really want to learn—or when he is cursed with a compulsion which learning cannot overcome. These are spiritual (not religious) matters alone.

While we cannot hope for perfection, we work for improvement, and then for excellence. Only the good can become excellent. I hear some talking of excellence who are not yet good. They should be trying to become better, not excellent. Excellence comes only to those who are capable of dedicating themselves to it. They are the ones who say, with Martha Graham, "When a student asks me whether they should dance, I tell them when they ask the question they've answered it . . . No."

As we climb the mountain toward the peak, the way gets narrower and steeper, and our need for a sure guide is greater. There are three areas as we move up the mountain which I feel require greater discipline. These are nobility of spirit, stability of emotion, and intellectual maturity. At this level, often each helps to mentor the other, for anyone dealing in these areas must maintain a strict personal discipline to retain what he teaches. These subjects cannot be taught by an outsider; they must be shown, lived, and developed in the exchange.

Traits of a Noble Spirit

In the nobility of the spirit we are talking about the transcendental part of man—the part that is too big to die. When my father died I wrote a friend, "I must believe in heaven for his spirit was too big not to be somewhere."

When John Donne wrote the lines "For whom the bell tolls" and "No man is an island," it was to lift up this feeling of nobility of spirit that included all mankind. It was to show his conviction that life is worth living, that no matter how low a man may go, there are still great heights to which he can aspire. Nobility of spirit goes far beyond a simple positive attitude or possibility thinking. These are good, but they are only the first step in reaching for the nobility of spirit—the true mystery of life, which is best expressed in poetry rather than prose.

Intellectual Maturity

The ultimate aim of intellectual development is the state of maturity in which understanding and wisdom combine. Wisdom is made up of the long view, the distillation of principles, the ability to choose wisely knowing that every opportunity is not a mandate. It also includes the willingness to make decisions—not just to be present where they are made, but to accept the responsibility for them.

Emotional Stability

Emotional stability does not necessarily give peace, joy, and a sound mind, but it does give the intellect and spirit an opportunity to work productively without being derailed by the emotions.

The eminent professor William James found "The greatest revolution in our generation is the discovery that human beings, by changing the inner attitudes of their minds, can change the outer aspects of their lives." Our emotions are the results of these attitudes.

We stabilize our emotions by lengthening our emotional wheelbase. The Cadillac rides better than a jeep because there is a longer time between the wheels hitting the bump. As we learn to stretch out our emotional reactions to the roughness of life, we automatically stabilize ourselves, like the difference between the emotion of a child and an adult. A baby has a short emotional base and can go from crying to laughing as quickly as it is pleased or displeased. Unfortunately, this is not too different from many adults I have dealt with. Make them happy and they smile; make them unhappy and they scream. They do not have the maturity to level out the emotions nor the control to minimize their reactions. A mature mentor can help.

The Top of the Mountain

If "just because it's there" is not reason enough to climb a mountain, few people will ever get to the top. A group was trudging up the mountain for the first time and one of them asked the seasoned guide, "Is it worth it?" To which he replied, "A higher view is always worth it." I'm reminded of the old hymn:

> Lord, lift me up and let me stand
> By faith on Heaven's tableland,
> A higher plane than I have found,
> Lord, lead me on to higher ground.

If we want higher ground, it is available through consistent, capable, dedicated mentoring.

In the remaining portion of this chapter, I want to tell you about one of my mentors who taught me by example through a life well lived.

MY MENTOR, MAXEY JARMAN

Maxey Jarman took a company from seventy-five employees to seventy-five thousand, making Genesco in the late sixties the world's largest apparel company, doing over a billion in sales. I joined him in 1941 when the company had five thousand employees and was doing less than one hundred million dollars. When reverses came, Maxey maintained a tremendous spiritual resiliency and kept contributing energetically, without bitterness, to many Christian causes. He was a man who rose to the very top in business, yet was uncompromising in his spiritual commitments. He inspired me in high times and in low times alike. He was always, for me, a living lesson.

I first met Maxey Jarman back in the mid-thirties when I was about twenty years old. I had been teaching a Sunday school class in a nurses' training program at Nashville General Hospital. One of the nurses became an industrial nurse, and she introduced me to her boss, the director of personnel. I said to myself, "I'd like a job like that." I had no training or experience, but I knew General Shoe (later Genesco) was one company in town where there might be such a position. So, I decided to meet Maxey Jarman, the president.

Maxey always bought gas at the station next to the plant. I waited until he drove up in his red Chrysler, then walked over and introduced myself. We just shook hands; he probably thought it was very strange, for in his early thirties he wasn't very gregarious.

Mary Alice and I had just married, and we were renting out one of our two bedrooms to a factory worker at General Shoe. When the renter told me of some labor problems at work, I called Mr. Jarman and offered my viewpoint. He invited me to his office. We had a short conversation, and I heard no more about it. But he impressed me so much that when I heard he taught a Sunday school class, I started attending. They had me lead singing and eventually elected me president of the class.

One Wednesday night after church in 1941, Maxey invited me to have a Coke at the Rexall drug store. We sat on fountain stools, and he asked me what I planned to do in life. "I'd like to be a personnel man," I told him. He asked if I'd ever had any experience, and I said, "No,

I've never even seen a personnel department. But I met a guy who's a personnel man, and I think I'd like that kind of work."

A Job Offer

That night I told Mary Alice I thought he would offer me a job, and no matter what he offered, I was going to take it because he was a man I wanted to be associated with. I sensed then I wanted to be with him for life. There was something significantly different about this man. Being a preacher's kid in the poor end of town, I'd become somewhat cynical about Christians. But Maxey personified reality. This was so valuable to me at that time. Here was a real man, a genuine person; and our years of friendship intensified that evaluation. When he offered me an opening in personnel, I was elated.

I had never seen a man so serious about wanting to reach the truth. For forty-three years I wrote my observations of Maxey on scraps of paper, everything from church bulletins to napkins, and last year I compiled them—five hundred pages of separate paragraphs. Then I spent three weeks at the lake doing little but reading them and thinking. When I told him about this, he said, "I'm amazed. What a waste of time!"

I've learned much from Maxey, but for this chapter I'll distill just a little. I started to say, "Some of these principles, perhaps, you will want to emulate." But Maxey would have been embarrassed to be held up as an example.

Maxey had an awesome *sense of responsibility*. He was not only involved, he was enveloped in what he did. He treated every responsibility as a "call," but never named it that. The Sunday night Maxey was taken to the hospital, barely able to breathe, he kept delaying because he was to speak at the evening service and "The pastor is counting on me." One of his favorite stories was of Jeb Stuart, who signed his letters to General Robert E. Lee, "Yours to count on." Occasionally, I would close my letters to him "YTCO." You could count on Maxey.

Cause-Oriented

Maxey was *cause-oriented.* He sublimated his ego and personal interests to whatever he was trying to accomplish. Most people simply cannot do that. Whatever he undertook, he did it "with all his might," from building the business to heading the committee for the revision of the King James Bible.

For instance, Maxey (Genesco) owned Tiffany Jewelry as a part of buying Bonwit Teller. When we'd go to restaurants in New York, people would look up and say, "There's Maxey Jarman who owns Tiffany." He enjoyed this connection with Tiffany, but then he sold it. I asked him why. "Because it doesn't fit our apparel company." Now, to sacrifice the ego satisfaction of being known as the man who owns Tiffany just to be more efficient for a larger responsibility requires dedication.

Maxey *thought little about himself.* His mind was occupied with opportunities and how he was going to get the job done. He thought of himself as little as anyone I've ever met. Most think of their private interests first, even when working for God. He didn't.

Maxey went through some painful problems; but because he wasn't self-centered, he didn't worry too much about being humiliated. As people have different thresholds of pain, Maxey had a different threshold of problem-bearing. Most humiliation is a reverse for our egos. Since Maxey didn't have the ego "high," he didn't experience the depths of the ego "low." He repeatedly quoted to me, "Be grateful for all things." I would say, *"In* all things." And he would repeat, *"For* all things." And on his prayer list of thanksgiving he had "when I'm being lied about." He oiled his effort with a deep joy and thanksgiving. Throughout his Bible, he repeatedly marked verses on joy and thanksgiving. On his personal prayer list he noted the things to be grateful for before he turned to problems and requests. Thanksgiving was a great part of his relationship with God. He had the humility of gratitude.

Future-Oriented

Maxey was *future-oriented.* He seldom wanted to reminisce. He would have been the poorest person in the world to attend a class reunion. Maxey was always looking to the future. Even in our last visit, while he was under the oxygen support system, going in and out of a light coma, he didn't reminisce; he wanted to talk about the black holes of space on which he was writing a paper, and a list of current world problems.

One of my prayers is: "Lord, give me a fresh today. I'm tired of dragging this yesterday around." Maxey, for some reason, was not cursed with this albatross.

Maxey believed in *progress, not perfection.* He criticized himself privately a great deal not because he failed to reach perfection, but because he wanted more progress. He realized that the difference in satisfactory progress and whimsical perfectionism is that perfectionism costs too much. There's a cover story in a recent issue of *Psychology Today* that shows the fallacies of perfectionism, and how often some people sacrifice broad progress for narrow perfection. Maxey avoided that.

Maxey *differentiated between gossip and grapevine.* He knew it was important to be on the grapevine and know what was going on. He wanted to be close to his people where it related to business. But he wasn't interested in gossip. I don't think I ever heard him whisper in his life. He made no effort to keep his voice low because he didn't maneuver you with confidences. If you said to Maxey, "I don't want you to breathe this," he would usually say, "Then don't tell it to me. It loads up my memory to remember what I'm not supposed to say."

Time

Time was Maxey's greatest "means." Since time was his greatest limitation, it was to be invested judiciously. He invested it in the cause that brought the highest return according to his priority list of responsibilities. He needed to feel at the end of the day he had fulfilled his greatest responsibility. In the office he was never chatty. His associates respected his time, yet he didn't rush about in a panic. His pace was fast and steady. He organized to save time, and was particularly short with telephone conversations—never rude, just businesslike. When he talked to you, he gave you his utmost attention, but you had the feeling that the subject should merit the time. I always wrote down what I wanted to talk to him about before I phoned. He never chided me into this; it was just that I felt in his attitude it was the courteous thing to do. Possibly he gave others this same feeling, for he was able to live without an unlisted phone number during all of his career. He always kept to the subject.

Maxey looked first at opportunities. No opportunity, no responsibility. You hear people bemoan the fact they can't meet a certain need. If you have no genuine opportunity, you have no responsibility. A man in jail can't become a foreign missionary. As Spurgeon said, "If you can't speak, God didn't call you to preach." Maxey had a great practical sense of what was possible.

Effort alone didn't count. He had limited regard for effort because he felt many people substitute effort for accomplishment. Some individuals feel that as soon as they're tired, they've done a good day's work. He respected *results* with the least possible effort. I never tried to impress Maxey with activity. I never told him how tired I was or how much I traveled. I accepted the rule, "Result is the best excuse for activity."

Maxey believed in people's potential. He realized most could do more than they thought; therefore he was always exploring ways to develop them. He studied motivation and tried many formal and informal methods. He preferred for people to pull responsibility to them, provided they would accept accountability for it.

He didn't see success for each person the same. In the mid-forties, one of our employees, Bill Fox, was killed in an automobile accident. I had just taken him off a machine and put him into the personnel department. As we drove back from the funeral, Maxey said, "I believe he was as successful a man as we have." I was completely taken aback by that. "What do you mean, Maxey?" His response was, "He did as much with what he had as anybody I know." Maxey considered anyone successful who maximized opportunity.

Discipline

Maxey implemented responsibility with a strong, consistent discipline. As responsibility was the reason for his work, so discipline was the method. Once I told him I was a person of few habits, to which he replied, "Then you must waste a lot of time." Habits were for saving time. He had habits for the routine things, and he reviewed them periodically to see if they were still helping him to be efficient. Those he didn't need he replaced, no matter how hard. Smoking was the toughest habit he ever tackled, but he broke it. Those things that could not be routinized into habits he listed on a priority sheet. Then he would work to complete the first item before tackling the second, wherever practical. He didn't jump around in his efforts. For example, he answered his mail as he read it—no shuffling through it two or three times. He went straight through his list for the day unless deterred by an emergency. He thought emergencies were the evidence of poor planning. Therefore he had very few.

His feeling of discipline was purely practical, not puritanical. He learned he could do more through strict discipline. He and Susannah Wesley would have been friends. Years ago, he shocked the Baptist brethren by admitting he worked on Sunday as a habit, not as an exception. He didn't push any ox into the ditch to justify working. He felt he should work, not waste time sleeping or reading the comics in the newspaper.

He went to church twice on Sundays and to Wednesday night prayer meetings. He read four chapters every day and five on Sunday to get him through the Bible once a year (over sixty times). He more than tithed, and he prayed daily. He taught two Bible classes, held most of the lay positions in his church, and served many other Christian organizations. As part of his discipline, he slept five and a half hours a night.

Competition

Competition was part of his discipline. He believed in it. Maxey never felt we could get the best from the organization until we had them under competition. He enjoyed setting up competition between departments and individuals. I thought of Maxey when I asked a world-class weightlifter how much more he could lift in a competition than he could in practice. He said, "About two hundred pounds." Maxey loved to argue, for it was verbal competition. We argued continually as a challenge. In fact, we often had to explain to strangers that we were friends.

Maxey was courteous, but still honest. Even in competitive business deals, he believed in helping anyone "save face" where there was no moral issue involved. He felt personal confrontations were unproductive. Maxey didn't want gunslingers in the organization—shooting either for him or against him. Even in the Christian community, Maxey was never one to make pious remarks such as "Bless you, brother," or volunteer to pray for you as a way of terminating a conversation. If he said, "I'll pray for you," that meant you went on a list. He had a daily, weekly, and monthly prayer list. He also kept a personal list of qualities for spiritual maturity he was praying about and developing in his own life.

Maxey was a catholic reader. He read constantly, quickly, and widely, usually five or six books at a time. Occasionally I would sit with him and another broadly educated person, exhilarated by the amazing conversation. The Bible and French history were his favorite subjects, and they led into a broad cross section of literature. He would read as many viewpoints as possible to help him form his opinion. He kept a large library, with much coming in and about the same amount going out. He had a rather low acquisitive drive. He discarded letters, records, files, and even books as they were used. The first book he ever suggested I read was Plutarch's *Lives.* He felt reading developed the mind as well as filled it.

Lists

Maxey made lists. The man who invented the pen deserves much of the credit for Maxey's contribution to life. Everything he wanted to do he wrote down. Each year he made a list of the things he was working into his personal development. To live was to improve, and to improve was to make a list for specificity. Once I was telling him some plans that he felt were fuzzy. He asked that I write him a memo on it. When I told him I couldn't write it but I could tell it to him, he smiled and said, "The only reason you can't write it is because you don't know it. Anything you know, you can write." That started me writing, and I believe he was right. As Bacon said, "Writing makes an exact man."

Maxey accepted his own weaknesses. For instance, his intuition about people wasn't exceptional. He accepted this and didn't waste time trying to develop skills he didn't have. He would say, "Don't try to strengthen people in their weaknesses; it's less productive than utilizing their strengths." The role of the organization was to free and synergize their strengths, and in some other way cover their weaknesses. He was good at recognizing talent and giving opportunity for its use—utilizing without "using" others.

Maxey never became cynical. He knew that to manage a large organization he had to trust his subordinates. The few who failed or conned him didn't change this conviction.

If you were to ask what satisfied Maxey most in all his accomplishments, I think it was the people he had helped develop by providing them opportunity. Once he told me, "It's not the plants we have built, but the people we have helped develop that makes me the proudest." A large part of his drive to expand the business was to provide opportunity for others. Geraldine Stutz, the owner of fabled Henri Bendel, told me at Maxey's funeral that when she bought the store, she immediately called Maxey and told him, "There is a Geraldine Stutz because there was a Maxey Jarman."

He had the normal temper ascribed to "redheads," but he controlled it well. When he did lose control, he was humiliated—not for social reasons, but because he lost his power to be effective. This was one of the few things that would upset him. Self-control was a matter of will, commanded by Scripture, and therefore his responsibility. In his Bible he defined *temperance* as "self-control." I felt he usually came nearer "righteous indignation" than hot-headedness. When I recall the times he was hot, it generally involved someone's irresponsibility or lying. He hated a lie. He couldn't understand anyone deliberately being dishonest.

Decisiveness

Maxey was decisive. This was one of his greatest leadership traits. He resented anyone "second guessing" his decision. He had an open mind before making a decision, but a very closed mind once that decision was made. Yet, I found he would quickly review a decision when he thought it involved a moral mistake. Once he had the books opened just to give an employee a $2.85 refund because "The question isn't how much trouble, but do we owe it?" Decisiveness, he felt, is one of the rarest traits in leadership. After he retired, he said, "Many people can make a good decision, but very few will." He wasn't a nervous leader; he had poise and tenacity.

Maxey was a much better demonstrator than a teacher. He rarely lectured; he showed you. He didn't do it to snow you or prove how capable he was. He simply did it, and you had to observe him to learn the lesson. In fact, you had to work with him to fully appreciate him. He was not colorful; he was effective. In following him, we felt we could do anything required without losing self-respect.

When we worked with Maxey, we could really "plant our feet" without looking over our shoulders expecting unethical maneuvers. He was loyal to his organization, and I never remember him making anyone a scapegoat. When I failed, he told me, but I knew he wouldn't sacrifice me to save his or anyone else's face. You just don't meet many people you can follow with that level of security.

Money to Maxey was a means, not an end. It's hard to think of Maxey without thinking of money because he handled so much of it. He was afraid of accumulating personal wealth. He talked about money's deception and the evils it brought to those obsessed by it. He proved his conviction by giving millions to Christian causes.

There were three facets to his giving that stand out to me. First, he gave currently. He didn't save up or wait for occasions. Second, he gave a very large percentage of his income. Tithing was much too little for him to give. Therefore, his personal fortune was always much less than it could have been. He gave it away. Third, Maxey believed in giving anonymously. He didn't want any earthly shrines named for him. In South America, Mary Alice and I were traveling with the Jarmans, visiting mission stations and churches. We repeatedly saw plaques denoting that the church had been given by Maxey Jarman. He never pointed out one of these, and I know he would have preferred the plaques not be there. Another time, I was visiting a preacher when he received, in the mail, a check for twenty-seven thousand dollars from Maxey—the answer to a request.

As close as we were, he never told me of a single gift he ever made, even though I know he offered as much as a million dollars to start a Bible school. He combined the wealth of the rich and the spirit of the widow's mite—but there were no trumpets blowing or the left hand telling the right what a great giver they belonged to.

Even when Maxey was at his lowest personal fortune, he gave a check for thirteen thousand dollars to help Youth for Christ with a project we were undertaking. It was the last of his mother's estate, which he had completely given away, just as he had given his inheritance from his father's estate to start the Jarman Foundation for Christian causes. During the darkest days of his temporary financial crunch, which he didn't try to hide or exploit, I asked him if he had ever thought of the millions he had given away. His answer was pure Jarmanese. "Of course I have, but remember, I didn't lose a penny I gave away. I only lost what I kept."

If Maxey were alive, I would never show him what I've written about him in this chapter. He would be embarrassed. I can almost see him push his lower lip over the upper and scowl. If I insisted, he would recognize my right to be wrong—"OK, if you think it will help, go ahead, but put some of my weaknesses in to balance it. You have said too many good things."

He built a billion-dollar corporation, but neither success nor failure were crucial to his interior life. He treated "those two impostors" just the same. Maxey Jarman was not a talking-teacher—he was a living example which made him one of my cherished mentors.

THINK ABOUT IT . . .

✗ A mentor's job is to create an environment for growth.

✗ When we stop learning, we stop living.

✗ "Men who know the same things are not profitable company for each other."

There are those who will never be able to stand alone, but through noble character they can aspire to lean lightly.

It takes time to turn information into knowledge and still more to turn it into wisdom.

Seeking counsel and seeking affirmation are two entirely different things.

Lesser humans crave acceptance, while greater ones seek accomplishment.

What you do best is probably so easy you underestimate its value.

The man who lifts heavy weights must take a broad stance.

growing in christ . . .

5

YOUR PEERS

Winning the Peer-Pressure Game

Peers come in groups. Seldom are they chosen individually. We move into a certain neighborhood. We go to work at a company where our associates come with the job, picked for us. When we join a church, a social or political group, we acquire peers, not by selection but by association.

Few of us escape peer pressure. Adults talk about its effect on young people but I find it everywhere. It never lets up—it simply takes a different form and uses a different rationalization with adults.

Those Chinese who were "in" when the Mao Tse-tung revolution took place used peer pressure to torture those who were "out" by excluding them. They took away their title, pointed their fingers at them, ignored them, gave them the silent treatment, completely ostracized them. The outsiders were dispossessed.

Some of the veterans of the Vietnam war feel they have been made outsider Americans. Often widows or wives after divorce feel this lostness, having no way to feel "in."

The evidences of peer pressure to be "in" dominate our styles in clothes. And even though we're not sure who sets them, we know when they're set and that peer groups will wear them. One young lady said she thought there was a monitor for designer labels in fashionable neighborhoods which set off an alarm when anybody came through the door without the right designer label on.

We prove we are "in" not only in the clothes, but in the slang we use. We appear knowledgeable and part of the group. Outdated slang is like outdated clothes.

Then there are the invitations that tell us if we are "in" or "out." The only thing some hate worse than cocktail parties is being left off the invitation list. Invitations of various sorts and functions define this inclusiveness in the group.

We have fads in sports, like tennis or golf. When tennis became the fad, people spent money on equipment and clothes to look like tennis players. They chased the ball after every hit, but they looked like "in" chasers.

Reading, for example, is also an evidence of being "in." The best seller list is accepted, even expected, conversation—it proves you read the right books. Entertainment serves much the same purpose, with the young people having to go to the rock concerts and moneyed people to the opera whether they like it or not. It's this being seen and being accepted that is so important. In-oriented youth grow into in-cultured adults.

Status Symbols

Status symbols become part of the peer pressure. A psychiatrist suggested he could become rich just by investing in the next status symbol. People not able to afford or accomplish these coming symbols become neurotics requiring psychiatric treatment. Look back if you will, and we see status symbols of the past: To own a home, to educate the kids, foreign travel, boats, winter vacations, and now it is second homes. In Christian circles, it's a trip to China and having your wife write a book. A wealthy lady living on Park Avenue told me she had several fur coats, but she had received each one when her husband wanted to squelch a rumor that his business wasn't doing well—furs and jewels offset financial rumors. How sad it was for her that these gifts had come as a result of rumors and not from love.

The best guide for handling peer pressure is from the Bible: "Be not conformed . . . but be transformed." A loose Smith paraphrase is, "Don't be molded from the outside (conformed) but have a set of values that forms you from the inside out (transformed)."

The Function Trap

Chaim Potok observed, ("No great man of letters is absorbed by the stream in which he swims.")This could be said of any profession. Too often I see people whose function has taken over their personage. Their job title is their description. When Roger Staubach was writing his excellent book, *Time Enough to Win,* he asked me in on the last chapter. He wanted to say something more than a great quarterback becomes a businessman. He wanted to say something about being a whole person. Roger was one of those highly talented, dedicated quarterbacks who knew that playing football was a function and was not his personage. Some fail to realize this, ending up their playing days making appearances, doing commercials, as "has beens." Early success in sports or entertainment can be a trap. The individual becomes a function and never learns to be a person.

Soon after retiring, the vice president of a corporation sank almost into a non-person. When he left his title, office, and organizational power, he had nothing left within himself. His power, his associations, his title, his activities were centered totally around his function, and he failed to realize that it was absorbing his persona. This can happen to mothers who quit being an individual and become only a mother. They forget the equally important function of being a wife and also of being an individual, so that when the children leave they have some reason to live. One husband told me his life at home was rather rough and when I asked him why he replied, "Our last child has just gone off to college and my wife has adopted me." His only hope was to pray that his children marry early and produce grandchildren to replace him. The mother function is one of the most noble and demanding; however, it should not become the total reason a woman lives.

In peer groups, certain things absorb people much as functions do. One of the most common expressions is, "This is living." Whenever I hear it, I try to correct it to say, "No, *I* am living." A particular style of living may be the most enjoyable we can know; but whether we have it or whether we don't, we are still living.

Responsibility to Peers

Having faced functions and things in peer groups, let's define our responsibility to our peers in terms of being an individualist and being redemptive:

My first responsibility is *to be an individualist.* Oftentimes when I'm lecturing to college students I will toy with them a bit by asking all those who feel that they are nonconformists to hold up their hands. Without fail, you get from 75 to 95 percent holding up their hands, and this immediately becomes funny to everybody who is thinking. Very few would admit that they were conformists because to be a nonconformist is part of the current philosophy. "Being me" seems to be defined as a maverick or a revolutionist, but never a conformist.

Actually, a conformist and nonconformist are the same personality types because they both are outside directed. They both form their opinion and behavior from where the "in" line is formed. The nonconformist wants to know where the line is so he *won't* be in it, just as the conformist wants to know where it is so he *will* be in it. In this respect, they are both the same types.

The value is in being an individualist who has a friendly attitude toward other people and would like to be a part of what they're doing, so long as they are right, not jeopardizing his set of values. He consistently hopes the group is right and will join them enthusiastically, but if they are wrong then he can either remove himself or challenge the cause they are espousing.

Our society today lays such heavy stress on "freedom." Permit me this observation: I would like to be an individualist and hope that most of the time I am, but I cannot accept the "free man" connotation of the individualist. So long as there is responsibility and death, there is no absolute freedom for the individual.

Some think freedom is tied up with money. As soon as you have enough money to tell people where to go you are free. This just isn't so. It isn't even true materialistically. When you are a prisoner of that attitude, you certainly are not free. Freedom is that we "accept causality with equanimity." The economist says there is "no such thing as a free lunch." Viktor Frankl says "ultimate freedom is man's right to choose his attitude." As we accept causality, we accept our right to choose attitude, occupation, relations, knowing full well we may be free to act but not free from the consequences of our act.

My second responsibility to peers is *to be redemptive* when and where I have opportunity. To be transformed is not just a personal thing, it is a starting point for the transformation of those around us, including the atmosphere or environment we create for others. The ultimate in redemptive action is to bring God's power to the people and situations in which we find ourselves. There is a sense in which to be redemptive is simply to replace evil with good, and that can be done religiously or philosophically by men of good manners and morals. Bringing God's power into

the situations in which we find ourselves is the true redemption of which the Scripture speaks.

The president of a bank recently had an experience
which has convinced him that Christ's spirit lives within
him. It has redeemed his very presence. Wherever he goes,
he is this power of redemption to his friends and, I'm
sure, to his associates. He has found to be true what Professor John Goodenough said when he became a Christian
as a professor at MIT, "The most powerful verse in the
Bible, to me, is 'Now you have the power to become.' "
He said he had always had an ethical sense of right and
wrong but had never felt the personal power to accomplish
it. This power came with an acceptance of the promise
at Pentecost: "You shall have power when the Spirit has
come upon you."

Being redemptive carries out the metaphors of the Christian life, such as light and salt. When we are light, we
create an environment for sight. Chasing away darkness
is not the main function of light, it is to provide an environment in which we can see clearly to encourage others and
to lead others in the rightness of life. This is why right
loves the light, for light is the environment in which it
functions best.

When we are called salt, we are a preservative in the
sense that we are anti-gossip, we refute error, and we pre-
serve the rightness of life. Also, as salt we flavor. As an
individualist I should have an improving, constructive personality, with friendliness and humor.

Disciplines of Redemption

Redemption requires discipline. First is the matter of
prayer. Personally I do not pray for miracles, but rather
for a willingness to join God in His process of working
out matters. Prayer is basically for me not to change God
nor to inform Him nor to convince Him to make me an
exception to His process. It is to make me conscious that

He is, that He is present, that He cares, and that His Spirit is available to dedicate us to the rightness of what we are doing. These benefits alone, if nothing else came from it, would make prayer very valuable.

We also bring redemption when we bring *the principles of the Bible* to whatever situation we are involved in, whether it's business, home, church, or social life. Too often the Bible is studied for its stories and its promises, not for its commands and principles. I believe that there is a genuine gift in delineating scriptural principles and that it is very expedient to study routinely someone who obviously has the ability to delineate these principles. Oswald Chambers, author of *My Utmost for His Highest,* has been one of my mentors in this area, as has Ray Stedman, one of America's great Bible teachers. It is so easy to get confused on the stories and not to get the genuine principle. For example, if we take the story of Daniel in the lion's den and extrapolate that into "whenever you do good God will not let harm come to you," then that does not square with the story of Stephen. It seems to me a better principle to say that we are to decide to do right and then let the consequences follow, whatever they may be. With Stephen it was stoning, with Daniel it was escape. Only a sovereign God knows which to let happen.

After I have prayed to be in a redemptive mood, equipped with biblical principles, then it becomes my responsibility to *face the day-to-day opportunities.* I am not one to grab lapels, nor am I gifted with evangelism, but I have found a very effective discipline which keeps me involved with others. Each morning if I will simply pray, "Lord, today I won't duck," that is all it takes. This simply means that I will discuss spiritual matters as easily and normally as I would any other matter. If a spiritual subject comes up, I discuss it, not duck it. Ducking one opportunity during the day cannot be made up for by volunteering to visit six people at night.

I believe only the Holy Spirit makes our witnessing effective and that those people whom I am supposed to affect come by me in a very natural sort of way—and as long as I don't duck, the witness will be effective. The temptation is to duck.

The Scripture says to Christians, "Take up your cross." God's redemption requires *death.* But this has gotten so dramatically involved with the suffering of the cross that I think sometimes when we talk about "taking up the cross" we are not talking about taking up redemption. For years, speakers have dramatically tried to stir up great emotion by describing the suffering of the cross. I believe that if Christ had died by lethal injection His death would have been just as redemptive as it was by crucifixion. Before you take up arms against me, remember that two others died with Him that day and evidently died a harder death because their legs had been broken. Christ did not short-cut his times by dying any way other than the normal way. He lived a normal life without sin, which is the miracle. He died not as an example but as a sacrifice, which is the power of His death. The story of the cross, to me, is not the story of suffering but of redemption.

Therefore, when a person is carrying his or her cross, it is not a matter of suffering, it's a matter of redemption. Wherever I bring Christ's power to redeem any situation, I am carrying my cross. It is not whether a child is sick, or a parent is senile, or I have had financial reverses. These things actually are nearer the thorn in the flesh which Paul suffered. I think in some ways we have mistaken the cross for the thorn.

At the moment of Christ's death man had reached his deepest depths, because he had, in disbelief, killed God, but at that same moment God had redeemed man and we were on our way to Easter. There can be no Easter without the cross—but the redemption and resurrection are the message we have to give, not the suffering. Human suffering can be redemptive to the person doing the suffering, such as John Bunyan in prison writing *Pilgrim's Progress* or Aleksandr Solzhenitsyn writing *Gulag Archipelago*. But suffering was not redemptive to Christ—He had no need of it. His life was always and eternally pure.

Peer pressure can be either a threat to conform us— or a challenge for us to be transformed. Either way, our peers are a formidable part of our human network. Through spiritual help we can win the peer-pressure game.

THINK ABOUT IT . . .

Unfortunately, as Emerson said, "We sip the foam of many lives."

Association with the best cools affection for the mediocre.

There is much to criticize in today's youth, but the most disgusting thing of all is that I am no longer one of them.

Those who say that we should love our neighbors as ourself, starting with ourself, generally find that they can spend enough time with themselves that they rarely get around to their neighbors. It should be added: "Love your neighbors at the same time you love yourself."

6

YOUR ENEMIES

They Really Can Be a Blessing

It is difficult to say, "Thank you, God, for enemies," but if we are to be thankful "in everything" then we have to be thankful for enemies. But why?

First, there is value in opposition. Nothing can make us evaluate ourselves more quickly or take stock more deeply than knowing that someone dislikes us. Fortunately, a lot of the good in the world has been done in response to the challenge of enemies.

Enemies are more than competitors or opponents as in games or business. They are persons who would kill part or all of us if they had the opportunity and could get away with it. Our enemies think the world would be better off without us. Sincere hostility is a trait of an enemy though correctness may not be. However, never dismiss an enemy without review and consideration.

A Command to Love

As a Christian we are never to be an enemy, rather we are commanded to love. Michael N. Hart, the historian, says that Christianity enjoys its greatest uniqueness in this, for no other great religion tells its adherents to love their enemies. In most religions, revenge is not only justified but commanded.

I believe God commands us to love our enemies because Christianity is a way of love and if we can love our enemies then we can love everyone. So long as there is anyone whom we cannot love, then our love is not complete. So long as we have not forgiven everyone, to that degree we cannot accept the forgiveness of God for ourselves. If we can love our enemies, then we have no difficulty believing God can love us. This relieves man, or at least gives him the possibility of relief, from one of his most damaging emotions—that of guilt.

The soul, once released from guilt, automatically exults, "I have been forgiven." This was the experience of Martin Luther, who was so conscious of his own sins that he would name them over and over. But he would still feel damned for a faulty memory that might have forgotten some he had not named. When he became convinced that he was saved by grace alone, he experienced such great relief for he felt forgiven. Then came the Reformation.

The father of the prodigal son brought the robe and ring and held festivities for him that he might believe that he had been forgiven. The son was forgiven before he got home, but only in the reception did he realize it.

Dr. James Cain of Mayo said a large part of the stomach trouble in America could be cured if people could forget the past. However, they can't forget the past because they haven't accepted forgiveness—neither their own nor God's. The apostle Paul dealt with it by saying, "Forgetting the things that are past." It is not "forgive and forget," but rather "be forgiven and forget."

In addition to strengthening our belief that God can love us, enemies increase our appreciation of security. Katherine Steele lost her artist husband and then a month later lost many of his well-known paintings when her house burned. In a personal letter she said, "Satan might as well give up for he is only making me snuggle closer to the Lord."

Enemies may threaten our security, our well-being, even our prosperity, but we see past them to the good that can come, which prompted Robert Browning to write, "Then welcome each rebuff that turns life's smoothness rough." Even Solzhenitsyn could be thankful for the "stinking straw" of his enemies that brought him to his maturity. Paul, fighting with the thorn in the flesh, still accepted it, knowing the value of opposition. When we see enemies as personified opposition, then we find a value in them. Through enemies we experience the sufficiency of God's grace in personal opposition. As someone said, "If all men were perfect, what then shall we have to tolerate from others for God's sake?"

Tough Love

Loving an enemy is not the sugary, sweet, syrupy love that most people talk about. It's a tough love—it's a disciplined love. It is the love that is best defined as "willing the ultimate good for the other person."

We are not commanded to agree with our enemies, for hopefully they are wrong, nor are we told to trust them, for they may not be trustworthy. Neither are we told to forget, for if we truly forgive them, we do not need to forget. The reason we say "forgive and forget" is because we feel that unless somebody forgets they have not forgiven. This is not necessarily practical among humans. As we remember another's tendency in the past, we are better able to keep him or her from making the same mistake again. It takes a very strict discipline to hate another's behavior without hating *him*. Then one asks, what can we hate? Steve Brown says it well: "We have the right to hate whatever God hates." And God hates wrong but not people.

The Power to Take Hurt

Furthermore, through enemies we learn to take hurt rather than give it and thereby redeem the situation. A young man in Peninsula Bible Church said, "If some dude is calling me names all over the street, I'm not going to try to understand him, I'm going to stop him. I'm going to grab him and push him down in the gutter." Then he paused and said, "I used to do that . . . I don't do it any more." He had found the power within himself to absorb injustice and discovered the power that a soft answer has to turn away wrath. This keeps the hostile situation from proliferating but also creates in the enemy's mind the question, "What gives him the power to do that?" This becomes, then, the witness to the spiritual power. For it is not natural to take hurt when you are perfectly capable of returning it.

The Catholic monk Thomas à Kempis said it this way, "It is good that we at times endure opposition and that we are evilly and untruly judged when our actions and intentions are good. Often such experiences promote humility and protect us from vainglory. For then we seek God's witness in the heart."

As we start to experience the superiority of divine good over evil, we can say with the clergyman who was robbed,

> Lord, I thank Thee
> First, because I was never robbed before;
> second, because although they took my purse,
> they did not take my life;
> third, although they took my all, it was not much;
> and fourth, because it was I who was robbed,
> and not I who robbed!

It may sound a little far out to say that the attacks of enemies open up opportunities for our help, but they do. Oftentimes a person will strike out almost aimlessly, not so much to hurt but to say, "I am hurting." His attack is his call for help. Jack Kerouac, one of the original beatniks, convinced me that much of the hostility toward God in the 1960s was really an attempt to find God. When he was asked what he was actually looking for, he surprised most of us by saying, "I am looking for God." He seemed willing to become an enemy of God so that God would strike him; he needed to know that He was there. Oftentimes we see this in children who, not receiving commendation for good behavior, act poorly, wanting at least attention for their bad behavior. These random strikes of ill will from people can open up to us their need.

Bearing an Enemy's Burden

The acid of enmity is a heavy burden. Being commanded to "bear each other's burdens," we bear an enemy's burden of hatred toward us as one way of helping them with their burden, for certainly hate is a burden. When I am with a man who dislikes me, I can forget his hatred of me as soon as I leave—but he has to carry it with him always. As I pray for him to have a lighter burden, I pray to have a lighter enemy.

Most of us, if given our wish, would choose to be more objective in our evaluation of people. We respect those who can truly and sanely differentiate between the strength and weakness of others. Nowhere are we tested more in this than in objectively evaluating our enemies. Look at wartime posters as an example. The enemy is always depicted as some kind of demeaned animal, leering out at God's people (us), with a mouth capable of eating human flesh. We forget that the posters in their homeland depict us the same way. Enemies are seldom objective, yet our enemies give us the opportunity to practice our objectivity at the point of greatest stress. Egypt's Anwar Sadat was able to do this and therein make his country's traditional enemy, Israel, an equal. This gave him a perfect platform for his great statement on peace: "There is no way to peace, for peace is the way." Without the enmity between Egypt and Israel, the press would not have thought the story newsworthy; but Sadat, by getting two old enemies together as new friends, astonished the world and the act received number one media coverage.

We develop maturity in the use we make of our enemies; not childishly denying that we have them, nor letting their opinion count so much with us that it keeps us from doing what we know we ought to do, but by working to make friends of them. Unfortunately, we Dale Carnegie-trained Christians have an inadequate view of enemies. We miss their value by writing them off as a liability.

Enemies Prevent Overconfidence

Enemies also serve another very subtle function. They keep us from developing too much confidence in our persuasive powers. A genuine con man never believes he has an enemy, or at least does not have one that he cannot persuade into being his friend. Just as it is healthy for those tempted by self-righteousness to come under attacks of temptation, so those inundated by their own persuasive confidence need an occasional enemy to prick their balloon. Otherwise, they develop more and more unethical maneuverability as a means of getting out of their problems. This eventually turns into pride, and I have on occasion actually seen it become criminal. I take some consolation in the adage, "Beware of him of whom all men speak well." Albert Lasker, the great advertising genius, said it this way, "Any man whom everybody defines the same way is wearing a mask."

Enemies are the opposite bank of our stream. They define our existence, often more nearly than we could or would do. Then use them for this value and work to make friends of them. We are advised, when possible, to live peacefully with all men—to be active peacemakers. None of us is so correct nor proper nor personable that the attack of any enemy cannot cause us to do some objective thinking about ourselves.

Reasons for Enmity toward Us

While we can avoid enmity toward others, we can't avoid all enmity toward us. Yet when we find we have an enemy, we can take a healthy review.

There are various reasons others dislike us. Here are a few:

1. *Our involvement in a cause can create enemies.* Once in the St. Moritz Hotel Cliff Barrows said to me, "We are getting along extremely well except there is always the offense of the Cross." I know few men who can claim as many friends as Cliff Barrows nor who deserve to have as many. Personally I cannot understand anyone not holding him in the highest respect, yet I do realize he represents, to some, the offense of the Cross.

Politically, we do not have total responsibility for enemies in war. These are for a cause, not of our own choosing but of our nation's choosing.

2. *Our differentness from others causes enemies.* Some people simply do not like anything "foreign." Paul faced this when he said, "I'll be all things to all men so that I might win some." He simply felt the responsibility to make an adjustment where he could morally. Once when I changed positions I found the plant that I had gone to was run by a different set of controls than I was familiar with, and it was my tendency to want to change to the system that I had been using. But I realized that all the people would have to change for my convenience. Therefore it was much more sensible that I change for their convenience. I think this is somewhat what Paul meant in the handling of differences. We are to dilute and work around our differences.

3. *Our self-centeredness can produce enemies.* We are selfish

by nature. In some ways that is extremely good, for it gives us a personal responsibility for ourselves. I have felt this is a great deal of the basis on which God judges us as individuals, because there is a certain disconnectedness among all of us that makes us unique. Yet one of the paradoxes of the faith is that we are to be servants of others rather than of ourselves. We are not to major on our unconnectedness—our not caring—our not being involved with others. We are told to divide our food, our clothes, and to use our time and talents in the service of others for the glory of God. I would not want this to be misinterpreted as agreeing with political welfare per se. I believe that we should: "Help where help is help."

Oftentimes help is actually not a help, and I say this having come from a very poor neighborhood. For example, in one Colorado town, I encountered families who have been on government relief for four generations. Too much government subsidy can destroy the will to work. It gets back to the definition of love: "Willing the ultimate good for the other person." Mere poverty aid is not the single criterion for testing the reality of the Christian's faith.

4. *Some enemies we make out of our aggression.* Man, according to Karl Menninger, may explain away 95 percent, or more, of all the things that used to be called sin, but there are two things that cannot be explained away. These are aggression and self-destruction. Aggression in this sense is simply the willingness, or even desire, to hurt another. We see it in our children, who naturally pick on a handicapped person. I have a brother to whose credit it can be said that he spent a good deal of his early life defending our handicapped brother. We have a carryover of the animal nature that simply is willing or desirous to hurt. Sometimes we call it practical joking, sometimes one-upmanship, and other times repartee. But whether socially acceptable or not, it is still aggression and is a way that many enemies are developed.

Psychologically we call it hostility. In the plant I have

seen older employees who felt that they were totally dependent on the company, becoming hostilely dependent—they
were dependent, and they were angry about it. Wives, as
they grow older, can face this same situation. This kind
of oppression or even a threatened oppression can result
in hostility, or aggression.

I hope after looking at some of the reasons others may
have for disliking us, we can see that the best use of our
enemies is to develop our forgiveness toward them. This
is the purification of our soul and develops our ability to
accept forgiveness in turn.

Becoming an enemy can be very harmful to us. First,
it can develop in us a spirit of revenge. Even such scientists
as Hans Selye warn us against revenge, for this is active
hate which, like fire, is never satisfied.

Then, too, no less an authority on war than Napoleon
warned us against continually fighting with our enemies.
"You must not fight too often with one enemy, for you
will teach him all your arts of war." Perhaps we will become
meaner than our meanest enemy. Often, this happens because if we feel justified in returning evil for evil, then
the evil grows larger and larger.

There is another excellent reason why we should avoid
being an enemy. Enemies make large psychological and
emotional investments in their enmity. Recently I was
speaking at a laymen's meeting. A father was in attendance
who has two handicapped children. Seemingly he had built
his life around this disaster, not being able to see any
blessing in the situation. At every opportunity he explained
the horror of his life as a result of having these mentally
retarded children. He has made such a huge psychological
investment over the years in this situation that I doubt if
he could ever accept his having taken the wrong attitude.
For him to believe he has made a mistake would be to
declare emotional bankruptcy.

Once a man exercised his hatred of another for many
years, thinking up reasons why his hate was justified. Being

justified in his own mind, he spread rumors of animosity about the person he hated. His health failed, but still he made this psychic investment without ever seeing or talking to the other person. Such hate is a losing psychic investment.

God does not want us making negative psychic investments in enmities. Therefore, we cannot treat another person as if he doesn't exist, for he does. To deny the situation is to deny truth. Instead we are to love the enemy; and as God loves the sinner and hates the sin, so we may be completely against the enemy's position or behavior, but not against the person. This demands love, for love is the thermometer of the soul.

THINK ABOUT IT . . .

"Be civil to all, sociable to many, familiar with few, friend to one, enemy to none." *Benjamin Franklin*

To update an old proverb, "If you're short of enemies, then lend money to some of your friends."

Anxiety, itself, is not all-important—what is important is what we do with the energy that anxiety creates.

Anger passes quickly for the wise and slowly for the fool.

Rejecting the Bible picture of man is no more effective than tearing up a photo of your enemy to get rid of him.

*why do we
suggest a friendship*

7

YOUR FRIENDS

Vital Buttresses for Our Lives

Friendship covers a broad range of relations, from the mildly pleasant to the intimate. Normal people have many friends counterbalanced by a few enemies. These friendships come on different levels.

The Anatomy of Friendship

1. *Our reservoir of friendship possibilities.* These are the friendly-looking folk. We nod at those who look friendly in a sort of recognition contract—we pass them often enough in the store to recognize and nod. They frequent the same restaurants and occasionally the same social or political group where there are too many activities and people to personally meet or seriously talk with anyone. However, they appear friendly, they have pleasant expressions on their faces, you know they would pick up something you dropped. They dress normally and might at some time have deferred to you going through a door. They are people you would be happy enough to know but not anxious enough to make the necessary effort.

2. *Friends of convenience.* Neighbors to whom we speak

140

but seldom talk seriously. Conveniently we receive packages for each other when out of town or pick up daily newspapers when away. They are "neighbors" either in our neighborhood, or they have the seats next to us in the stadium or at the concert. We ask each other, "How are you?" and are willing to listen briefly. But we appreciate it if they realize the question is more courtesy than interest. As friends of convenience, we are happy enough to speak but not close enough to borrow.

3. *Friends of mutuality.* Will McGrath, chairman of Williamson Company, taught me "friendship in business is mutual advantage." When either stops enjoying an advantage, the friendship dies. I felt, as a young man coming into management, this was a cynical approach; in maturity, however, I have found it completely reliable. For friendship to live beyond the advantage, it has to become deeper than an exchange of favor, benefits, and profits. In the long years since Will told me that, I've had occasion to warn many of my retiring executive friends they would experience a change in relationship with "friends of mutual advantage" and not to become bitter or disillusioned.

We all prefer to think people like us for ourselves and not for our gifts or benefits to them—but this is a little naive. Men who retire as the head of a corporation and have been accustomed to having their telephone calls returned immediately find this just doesn't happen. One of them told me that he had learned not to leave his telephone number, but simply to call back until he reached the person because he didn't like to be embarrassed by not having the phone call returned. The chief executive officer of a large corporation retired to Florida in a most exclusive condominium. Then he refused to attend his second owners' meeting for, his wife said, he complained that nobody listened when he talked. It was a new and unpleasant experience. Women who relinquish prominent social positions face this same situation. Professionally, no one loses more personal power than a society reporter who changes jobs.

Actually, in these circumstances of "mutual advantage," we are friends of the function, not of the person—better to say that our functions are friends of each other. When that function ceases it is as if we had died with the demise of the function.

Large donors who have financial reverses experience this loss of attention and prestige. Donors are appreciated for what they can give, not for what they have given. Perhaps gratitude is the most fragile emotion. Recently a religious fund-raiser, when I told him I was not going to make a contribution, changed his whole attitude. He divided people between those who were going to give and those who were not. He did not waste his limited friendly attention on the nongiver but lavished it on the current giver.

4. *Period friendships.* Members of the same team or the same active organization are friends for a period—"for the duration." We are birds of a feather flocking together for a common purpose. This shows in a class reunion where those who once felt so close to each other are now alienated by time. Each pokes around with a few curious questions and either gloats or envies as they relate their wins and losses. Voted the class fool, the rich come back in their fancy cars to prove they have done well, and the ugly girl brings her husband, telling about her lovely children. A few naturally friendly, caring personalities tie up the lost chords and manage to play a few harmonies of genuinely worthwhile music.

In period friendship, fanatical friendships often develop, such as in political and religious societies where it is at most a sin or at least a misdemeanor not to profess closeness, almost blood-relatedness, with the others. In a sense, these period relationships prove Eric Hoffer's theory of "the true believer" where people give over their wills to the movement. Such friendships by association are truly dangerous, for strangers in the white heat of fanaticism become friends of the cause—but for a period only.

The Deeper Friendships Relate to Love

Meaningful friendship is a narrow level—the small tip at the top of the acquaintance pyramid reserved for "real" friends.

Lasting friendship and love relations, while different, still share some common ground which needs recognition. Friendship is often more comfortable than love. It gives more breathing room. It doesn't have the love-hate elements that most love affairs have. It leaves each individual an entity—touching but not having been made one. It doesn't concretize togetherness. Neither does it have the high and low emotions that belong to love. A spouse can get angrier at a mate than at a friend, but then love wins over hate and sends roses to a lover and not to a friend.

Friendship is more flexible, less time-consuming than a love relationship. Lovers compulsively want to be together. Friends can relax even though apart. Often friends carry on an imaginary conversation without the other even being present. It isn't insanity—it's rapport—empathy. We know what the other *would* say, but still we want to hear them say it, if only in our minds. We carry a memory of their voice and way of thinking.

Love and friendship can't be fully compared—yet they do compare themselves by their very presence in each of us. We have both love and friendship relations, each with a high claim on the emotions. At times both seem to cohabit the same cells of the mind and heart. At other times they seem strangers in the same house.

Between the sexes a healthy, respectful friendship can be the start of a healthy love. Yet some couples miss a lot by loving without ever being friends. Unfortunately, married couples sometimes stop being friends. As a divorce lawyer said to me, "Often a divorce is caused simply because the two have stopped being friends." They became competitors, seeing each other as inhibitors and deprivers of what might have been. Unfortunately, some young people live together without marriage hoping to keep friendship as well as love. If they saw more marriages in which love and friendship grew together, they would be willing to make the complete commitment to both.

Definition of Love

Frankly, I do not know of a good, concise, precise definition of the love which includes physical, mental, emotional, and spiritual elements. Even the ancient and wise Greeks used four words for love where we use one. Love is so poorly understood. Here's the best definition I know, and it fits equally well with lovers and friends: "Love is willing the ultimate good for the other person."

Love is deeply involved in the will. Love, if left entirely to feelings, invariably ends up being selfish. Being naturally selfish, without the discipline of will, love will not stay central on "the ultimate good of the other." It becomes *my* ultimate above *thy* ultimate. When I hear someone badger another with "if you loved me you would . . .", I suspect selfishness rather than love.

This definition gives love two measurable and controllable elements: will and ultimate good. This provides the basis for maturely reacting to the other person against our own selfish emotions, even those of sex. By looking at the term "ultimate good," we are able to include discipline, restraint, and even confrontation in our reactions to the other person.

Dr. Barbara Brown is doing some fascinating research in biochemistry, determining the effect of will by psychological and physiological experiments. One of these days, I believe, science is going to prove that the essence of man is his will. Good and evil both pipe to it. In the humanities it's positive and negative—in philosophy it's good and evil—and in religion it's God and Satan.

The Evolution of Friendship

There have been cases where people fell in love at first sight. I know of no deep friendships that have been born with this suddenness. Graphically, I see friendship as two contiguous circles, each of which has a smaller circle inside. The outer circle symbolizes the adult and the inner circle the child inside the adult. The outer circles represent acquaintanceship between adults. Whether this relationship becomes good friends or good acquaintances is determined by the child inside the adult, for psychologists and our spouses have always known that inside of each of us is still a little child. Many times he runs the show—particularly in deep relationships.

This totally unvalidated, unscientific approach to analyzing friendship has led me to believe that real friendship happens after two adults become pleasantly acquainted (the outer circles). Then the two children inside get to liking each other. Adults will often say, "Yes, I know him—he is my good friend." The child inside us would come nearer saying, "Yes, I know him, and I am his good friend." It is reminiscent of Mr. H. L. Hunt asking me, during a Laymen's Leadership Institute, to call him. When I called, his secretary wisely asked, "Does Mr. Hunt know you?" It does make a difference who does the knowing.

This evolution of friendship is an interesting process to watch, even though it is seldom completed. It is started often, yes—but seldom finished. For example, two men meet, get acquainted, and begin to like each other. They like each other as men and therefore do not become too close at first. Each guards his image and his interest but feels drawn to the other. Each suspects that if they could get closer they would like each other even better, and so they start the process of introducing the two boys inside them. For many, liquor serves the purpose. The men drink together and become less inhibited. They start to remove part of the masculine fence and let the boys get a chance to meet each other. They go fishing, play games, or travel together, gradually taking down one paling of the fence after the other, slowly, in limited areas. I have seen small prayer groups serve this same function for individuals.

Where the little guys seem to like each other in the opened areas, the two men keep opening until they have been able to remove more and more of the fence. If they find the two little boys are starting to dislike each other, then the men start rebuilding the fence. Where liquor is involved they invariably say, "I was drinking—it wasn't me." The opposite, of course, is true. At other times, "I was joking, of course," starts the fence rebuilding.

This fence is symbolic of the masculine image which all of us maintain to some degree or other. Though none of us have a total mask, few of us are totally without some mask.

The Importance of Masks

This masked area is crucial in friendship relations. It is the one that must be understood and appreciated, even if not agreed with. Obviously, none of us are satisfied with the masked area of our lives, and we are careful in allowing anyone to see behind the mask. We feel sensitive, hurt, even guilty, and we are afraid for others to see or know. We wonder about their reactions. Until we can predict their reactions, we are unable to become close friends.

Our mask is protective, like a bandage. The larger the mask or the more complicated, the more painful the area which it protects. These are our lonely areas, the parts we know ourselves. We may even have accepted them but think others do not know and, worse still, would not accept them. Some are caused by wounds. Others are birthmarks. Since neither is satisfactory to us, we cover them up with a bandage or a mask.

In the early stages of what will become a genuine experience in friendship comes the almost sacred moments when the masked area is shown or rather, is "permitted to be seen." At first, a "chance" remark or often a humorous reference or remark of similarity alludes to it. This lightly lifts or slightly shifts the mask. This first moment of admission has a particular intimacy about it. At its best empathy should not belittle the other person's evaluation of the need. The wounded read very carefully the reaction of another. With encouragement and understanding, the willingness to lift the mask grows.

Psychiatrists have given us the helpful understanding of "body image" in which everything is included that the person holds within his picture of himself. Often the mask is part of that "real you" and cannot be brutalized by "using a hatchet to kill a fly on a friend's forehead." The mask is not only real, just as bandages are real, but it is usually very much needed. Getting rid of a mask too quickly can be disastrous for the person and the relationship. Unfortunately, I've seen well-meaning people try to tear off someone's mask without the sensitivity to realize the skin or the soul was attached. While they could tear off the mask, they couldn't stop the bleeding or erase the scar.

Most masks are not hypocritical. Is a bandage hypocritical? Is it wrong to make it the color of flesh so it won't stand out? I think not. A man may wear a patch over a bad eye to protect others from the unpleasantness. He has grown accustomed to the eye. The sight of it doesn't shake him at all, but he knows it may shake others; therefore, he wears a patch. Bless him—not as a hypocrite but as a humanitarian.

More of us should hide our unpleasantness under a courtesy patch. Etiquette in social life is to hide our naturally unpleasant dispositions. Be thankful for it.

The Hypocritical Image

The hypocritical image or mask on the other hand, is created to make a person appear to be what he has no

real desire to be. The pious look of self-righteousness—
the plastic smile of the insincere. These want credit for
what they are not willing to do or be. Call them what
they are—con men.

The man who wears elevator shoes isn't a hypocrite.
He genuinely would like to be taller. Why deny him this
assistance in standing eye to eye? The padded shoulders
are bought by the man who would rather have big shoulders than big pads. These are assists in comfort, not
practices in hypocrisy. Let sufferers be whole, even if temporarily.

Masks, even those best constructed, do have their pen-
alty. They create loneliness. They isolate the areas of discontent with our own lives and being. They identify the
parts we don't want exposed constantly. Real friendship
shares this loneliness. Friendship not only says it understands—it does. Its behavior understands. Its mindset and
ways of thinking understand. Its reflexes understand.
Friendship somehow feels the person is greater for bearing
the handicap. Therefore the handicap becomes a plus, not
a minus, to a friend.

Beware the Sudden Share

Continuing responsibility is the flesh and bone of friendship. I have seen some good in the religious small groups,
but I've also seen some real danger. Such groups have
been beneficial to many and have a real place. But there
is a subtle danger where people try to get out from under-
neath loneliness by sharing the very thing which will later
isolate them from the group. What made them lonely, when
 shared, will eventually make it difficult for them to face
the very people with whom they shared. Then they will
be sorry they confided in someone who had no deep friendship for them.

For example, one night someone was making a case for
small group confession by telling about a couple who, on

their first visit, became warmed by the fellowship and admitted they had lived together for two years before getting married. I'm afraid this couple will be sorry they told that. I heard it secondhand and others will hear it in the same way. It could eventually exclude the couple from the fellowship they tried to gain, rather than making them part of it. I fault leadership that encourages this type of exposure. It's a dangerous practice.

Sharing is the privilege of friendship, but I sometimes suspect the word "share" has been overworked. Too often, the person is saying in reality, "Let me slip up on you" or "It's show-and-tell time." The immature or emotionally disturbed rush into this trap, not being able to find a way out.

Personal confidences are for friends—the tried and true ones. Spanish philosopher Baltasar Gracian said it well: "Never give a pawn on your honor until you have one on his." This is more practical than cynical.

Friends Are Made Slowly—Enemies Quickly

The perverseness of our nature helps us to make enemies very quickly. It would be wonderful if the making of enemies were as slow a process as the making of friends. It is not, and so we accept the fact.

The Dignity in Friendship

Friendships, to be real, need not be casual, informal, buddy-buddy stuff. Throughout, some friendships retain their dignity, almost a formality, yet are no less real. I am thinking of my dear friend Dr. Gumperz who, for seventeen years, was a close, close friend. I probably have the only signed picture he ever gave to anyone. Yet throughout he always retained a scholarly aloofness. By nature he was an introvert, by profession a scholar. To me, he was always *Dr.* Gumperz—never did I use his given name in all the seventeen years of close association. Yet we cared for each other. No matter how busy, I could always reach him. Our conversations involved each other's ultimate welfare but none of the small minutiae that used up the time he could be using better as my mentor. It is almost impossible for me to realize that in those seventeen years of close association I have never known whether or not he had children. On one occasion I met his wife, a charming actress from England, and I saw that we shared the same reverence for him. When the New York papers carried his obituary, they said, "The awesome intellect of Dr. Gumperz is gone." It is not, and never will be so long as those of us who profited from knowing him are still alive. It is the human immortality of friendship.

Repeatedly, Maxey Jarman asked me to call him Maxey, but it just didn't seem to describe my respect for him and so, for many years, I waited until calling him by his first name was natural. Agewise we were eleven years apart and yet, though both adults, it was the man and not his age which drew my respect. There is a great element of respect in friendship.

Frankly, I resent too much early intimacy before friendship has taken deep root.

Most close friends really respect the other's character and generally like his or her personality—even if it is a little flaky. Even the character can be flawed, as it is with most of us. A friend understands the flaw and is able to relate around it. The personality may seem strange, but it is understandable to the friend. I do not understand how such understanding happens. I only know it is necessary in friendship.

Too Much to Ask of Friendship

Friendship cannot rid us of all loneliness. That is asking too much. Individuals of depth, meaning, sensitivity, and complexity are all lonely at times. In this loneliness we become aware of our individuality, uniqueness, and exclusive responsibility. Leaders learn early that the price of leadership is loneliness.

I remember sitting on a boat dock in the early, misty morning listening to Bill Mead's plans for his corporation. I still feel the joy of sharing that thinking but also the feeling of not being able to share his ultimate responsibility. I was there, but he was also alone. Friendship did what it could, but there are things friendship cannot do without harming the friend. Bill didn't need or ask me to make his decisions. I only helped create an environment in which he could make them most comfortably.

Once, riding through Kentucky with Howard Butt, Jr., a deeply spiritual friend, I had this same, almost mystical experience. We were talking and, slowly, as if by rheostat, he became quiet. Then, as if alone, he began to sing an old hymn. In this high moment I saw him and God so physically together. Each of us was alone yet sharing our aloneness in deepest friendship. We cannot and should not disdain or neglect our aloneness.

Interested, But Not Curious

The deep, sincere interest in each other as friends does not include curiosity. Personally, I'm "turned off" by people who are curious about me. Interested, yes; curious, no. Often people confuse interest in people with curiosity about people. Most news tabloids promote curiosity rather than interest. Interest has a positive, helpful, outgoing connotation. Curiosity is self-centered. Seeing and hearing about a person can scratch the curiosity itch, while interest requires affirmative effort with desire to do good plus good will toward the person. These are a hundred and eighty degrees apart.

Since curiosity is natural in most of us, it must be bridled in friendship. No doubt you have noticed how curiosity shows up in the type of questions that are asked. If wives stopped asking curious questions, most executives would talk more about the business at home. He's happy to answer interested questions but not curious ones. Curious questions show willingness to probe for selfish reasons— to accuse, to insinuate, and to threaten. Television interviews show the threat is very effective many times in prising out information. All of these techniques, when used by friend or spouse, simply train the other to keep quiet.

Friendship demands the willingness to have a question go unanswered or, even more, a question go unasked. There are friends who have situations about which I am curious and have been for years. I haven't asked certain questions, because they would be curiosity questions. Therefore I wait. Curiosity can frostbite a budding friendship.

There are areas of privacy in all of our lives which must be protected. I doubt that I could fully respect anyone who wanted to expose their complete life without areas of privacy. Their judgment as well as their taste would be flawed. For example, marital sex relations is simply an area which remains personal until there is an overwhelming reason or natural situation for discussion.

Money is generally a private subject. I have no desire to know the exact worth of any of my friends and only one has ever told me. Then it was a matter that he wanted to discuss with the view to taking a speculative chance. We discussed it this once and never again. It is offensive to ask someone their worth. Privacy should not be invaded, even by a friend. Friendship is a disciplined relation, and its great freedom comes from the natural dignity that friends maintain.

Serve Their Loneliness

A spouse should allow the other "bragging time." Generally the husband needs it more than the wife, particularly if he is in a constantly competitive environment. A person gets beaten down and needs to get the balloon inflated again. This is why "bragging time" is important. Without someone to share our successes, we get very lonely. Once a very knowledgeable young woman told me nearly any husband whose wife will not listen to and encourage his bragging is vulnerable to another woman. We need to know someone thinks we are good.

Once I complimented George Beverly Shea on his singing at Billy Graham's birthday party, and he pensively said, "This is when I miss Erma, I would like to tell her." In that little sentence I understood much of the greatness of Erma and Bev's relationship.

Friends of Friends Aren't Friends

There is a protection we owe our friends against intrusion from others, even our other friends. When it became known that Maxey Jarman was going to sell Tiffany, I was surprised to find how many "friends" I had who wanted to make a deal. I had to be blunt because I owed him protection as part of our friendship.

Actually, the arithmetic works against friends of friends being friends. If we are lucky, maybe one person in a thousand acquaintances becomes a close friend. It is staggering to think of the coincidence that two out of two would become friends with two different people. A duet can seldom be turned into a trio just because one person would like to see it happen. We must give our friends the option of not being friends with our friends.

The Protection for Friends

Friends must feel they are safe from being used by the other. Recently in a business seminar I mentioned a few well-respected individuals with whom I had shared a meaningful relationship. One of the executives attending asked me how I had been able to have such influential friends.

He didn't strike me as an individual to whom I felt any great informational obligation, and I was not sure I could trust much delicate information with him. Therefore I said, "First, a friend must know that he will never be manipulated for selfish interests." His wife nudged him, saying, "Listen." Then I knew why he had been so quick to ask the question.

Unfortunately, as we mature and our friends come into power, they find that they are very limited in the new friends they can trust, and so they must stick to the old ones. Often I have seen them become almost cynical about making new ones, for time after time these new friends had tried to maneuver for their own advantage. Some took longer than others to show their selfish interests. The percentage was discouraging.

Friends Require Time

Friendships cost time, thought, and effort. Any relationship requires nurturing. We don't really think too much about it in friendship because we enjoy doing the things that keep it healthy. It's like thinking of work as not being work when we really enjoy doing it. Remember the old saying, "Work is what I'm doing when I'd rather be doing something else."

It's not just the time that friends are together that counts. We must also take into account the time we are asked to give to their requests. An executive once told me he couldn't allow himself to have too many friends. He knew they would make heavy demands on his time. His time was too scarce.

Character Evaluated

Increasingly I realized that friendship cannot really be established until each feels that he has properly evaluated the other's character. I'm not saying men of poor character cannot be good friends. There have been many. Neither am I saying all men of good character can become close friends. Men of excellent character sometimes can't abide each other personally. I am convinced, however, that friendship involves an evaluation of character—good, bad, or otherwise. Each must know where the potholes are and find a reasonable rationale for them. Each must know the other well enough to feel that he can predict actions as well as understand reactions.

Knowing and respecting the other's motive is the first requirement in evaluating his character. To misread motives is a sure sign of an imperfect evaluation of character, and distrust will follow. While in Europe I was talking to an American psychiatrist about another psychiatrist. When I mentioned the other's name, the first psychiatrist really took off on him. In fact, he went overboard in saying, "When he dies, he's so crooked they will screw him into the ground." I knew this wasn't true, but I also knew the psychiatrist with whom I was talking was a man of integrity, with very little natural hostility. Therefore, I asked him to make another check to see if this really were his correct evaluation. The next day he came, very shaken and almost with tears, saying that he was wrong—he had mistaken two men because they had both held the same position and had similar names.

I felt a surge of strength in my friendship for the absent psychiatrist because I realized I could spot evaluations uncharacteristic of him.

We can never be comfortable with someone whom we feel evaluates our character or motives improperly. Occasionally, when someone predicts that a person will do such and so, I would like to say, "But that is not according to his character—his words, as well as his behavior, say 'that is not me.'" Often, when I am criticized, I would like to say the same thing in defense of myself.

There are some things which may be done as an exception and should be recognized as such. Though it takes time and a lot of living together to get to this point of truly evaluating each other's character, it is one of the rewards of friendship. In real friendship, there are very few great surprises.

Keeping Confidences

Strong friendship involves confidences. Without confidences, there cannot be genuine friendship. The giving and receiving of confidences is really the test of friendship. We grow in proportion to the size of our confidences which we exchange. This shows we trust each other, and for this reason friendships normally grow very slowly. Within all of us is this deep desire to be known—but not the same willingness. We would like to know more people than we would like to know us. I mean really *know*. Oftentimes we want temporary association but not permanent, and this is the stuff of which prostitution is made.

By empathy we feel the depth of interest each has in a subject and, until we know that depth, it is dangerous to share confidential matters. I have known some people who resented having to discipline themselves to keep confidences and much preferred not knowing anything in confidence. In fact, they asked that they not be given anything which they had to keep, simply because it utilized too much mental effort to protect it. Others, of course, of a much meaner nature use these confidences to feed their rumor mill and as a ticket to get into gossip groups.

Until friends are able to feel the depth of interest each has in the subject, it is impossible for the one who hears the confidence to know how important it is to the one giving it. If he fails to grasp its importance and remember to safeguard it, then he will let it slip out, not maliciously but just because it didn't register with him as that important. There must be a commitment to keeping confidences—one must feel with depth what the other feels about the matter. In that way we maintain a view of confi-

dence for each other that is the same as we have for ourselves. What is important to one is important to the other;
consequently, it sets up on our emotional grid that way.

Mutual Irritations

Friendships can break up over dissimilar dislikes as well
as over the lack of similarities. Our irritating traits and
our contrary opinions demand tolerance, each from the
other. If this tolerance is not given, then there comes an
irritation in the friendship that eventually drives the two
apart. Often such irritations keep friendships from forming
which otherwise would.

Often an individual who becomes fanatical on a subject
will insist his friends share his new-found fanaticism. This
can strain a perfectly good friendship. Even physical annoy-
ances affect friendship. Once I took a trip with a man who
sniffed all the time. I tried to pick up his cadence—it still
bothered me. I tried to analyze the difference in volume,
but no matter how much I tried to turn the experience
into an experiment, it still was an experience—a most un-
nerving one.

Or yet is there anything worse than trying to travel with
someone who is eternally tardy? A small matter to some,
but I am convinced such an irritation can prevent a friendship from developing.

Even driving erratically can put too great a strain on
the nerves for togetherness. Once we went on a trip to
east Tennessee with a couple who made a wreck of us.
He would vary his driving on the highway as much as thirty
miles an hour—fast and slow—up and down. I was ready
to scream but couldn't.

I remember one fellow laughed so loudly in public no
one wanted to be out with him. We probably could go
on naming small irritations, but probably the one which
gets to us without being defined often enough is an allergy
to silence. These people don't know when to be quiet.

For example, a nonfan of football can ruin the Super Bowl by talking about anything and everything else while the game is on.

One of the emotions most difficult to tolerate is embarrassment. It's hard to know what will embarrass each of us but there are definite things. My poor, uncoordinated dressing was an embarrassment to some. They had rather leave me at home than take me.

When such irritating habits develop after the friendship is well matured, it may be tolerated, for friendship has a way of developing mutual tolerances.

As irritating as personal habits are, misunderstood opinions are worse. For example, when one friend becomes a fanatic in some political persuasion or religious belief, the other simply may not be able to abide that change nor want to be under the constant bombardment of his friend's new "magnificent obsession."

Occasionally I've seen lifelong friendships form basically on sharing some fanatical opinion, particularly when their opinion is hostile to some organization or other group. They bask and relax in their hostility and incrimination of the others. It seems to draw them together in much the same way as an outside foe draws a nation together. If, however, one were to change his opinion of that practice, it would drive a real wedge into the friendship.

Test of Friendship

Someone jokingly, though not totally facetiously, said that you can tell a real friend when you call him from jail. If he asks "Where?" he's your friend. If he asks "Why?" he isn't.

Seriously, there are some reliable tests of friendship. One of these is to ask how the relationship stands separation. Friends, once they have become deeply involved with each other, can be apart for months or even years and then, after five minutes together, it's as if they had never been separated. They seem to have been running along parallel tracks, even when apart. They're really interested in each other as persons, not in impressing each other. So when they do get together, they spend their time catching up, not competing.

Another characteristic of friendship above acquaintance-ship is the genuine desire of friends to help each other. They really want the other to do well and are happy to contribute to that welfare. Friends look for ways to help each other. They think of each other when opportunities arise.

The greatest test of friendship is not sharing failures but sharing success. It takes real friendship to be happy to see the other person do better than we have done. I'm talking about the kind of success in which we cannot even share or from which we cannot gain. Genuinely enjoying the other's success proves the sincerity of the friendship.

We should wish our friends success and let it come from any source. If someone is able to help them more than we can, then we should continue to contribute our minor part graciously. Parents are faced with this situation as their children approach adulthood.

In real friendship we are happy to see the other person do better than we. This was really the secret of David and Jonathan's friendship. Jonathan was the rightful heir to the throne, but he knew that God had appointed David. He rejoiced in this and joined in his anointing enthusiastically, even though it meant David replaced him. This was what he understood to be "esteeming the other more highly than yourself."

While it is good to have sympathy for friends, it's better to have praise. I didn't say it was easier. It's easy to sympathize, because we are generally better off than the one with whom we sympathize. In success we're tempted to envy others—to ask what they have done that we haven't—

to suspect them of having the "big head," and to indulge in all those kinds of selfish thoughts which have no place in friendship.

Another test is that friends are able to communicate without preface to their conversation. They don't apologize or maneuver for a favorable position in the conversation. Diplomacy is not part of the language of friendship. Diplomacy is the language of manipulation. Certainly there is consideration, but very little preface. There is an assumed integrity in friendship communications.

No Jealousy in Friendship

Children, in their immaturity, developing their first friends, seed them as if they were players in a tennis tournament. They know exactly who their best friend is, and they have to know they are first on the other person's list also. Therefore, another test of mature friendship is that each is happy to see the other form close friendships with others. There is no jealousy. Each is happy to be one among many, not demanding exclusivity.

We enjoy seeing other friendships involving our friends. We appreciate the necessity of sharing time and attention which we may have held exclusively. Often it means listening to an account of an experience that we are not part of, and we must discipline ourselves not to try to match or "top" experience for experience. This is *willing the best for the other.*

Sometimes I see the guests on Johnny Carson's show moving from the number one seat down the line and think of people trying to set up their friends in the same kind of rotation. Friends expect and understand that sometimes the current interest of the other person keeps them from spending as much time together as usual.

The most self-sacrificing aspect of any genuine friendship is that either party is willing for the friendship to go dormant if it is for the other's ultimate good. This is difficult to understand and harder to accept. It isn't that the friendship has died, it simply must by agreement become dormant. This requires probably the most mature attitude of any other aspect of friendship.

Another test is the willingness to say no to each other. This one is not comfortable but essential. There must always be this feeling of controlling your own life to the point that not even a close friend can take over that control. Friends are not copilots in a plane with each being able to take over the controls at any time for both. That is demeaning and irresponsible.

"Yours to Count On"

Friendships can't be forced. Sometimes, unfortunately, friendship just doesn't happen. We know individuals who are really not our friends. We wish they were. We may spend lots of time together—have lots of mutual interests—we may be able to communicate well and even to share confidences in limited areas. However, if the chips were down, the friendship would not stand. A friend has to be one to "count on."

The last test of friendship I will mention is the humor in friendship. We know a man's character by his ability to laugh at himself, and we know a friendship by our ability to laugh at each other. There is no derision, simply the acceptance of imperfection that each recognizes in the other. Oftentimes the very existence of the friendship is the basis of humor. These are the friendships which prompt questions like "Why should two people like us, so much alike and yet so different, care so much for each other?"

Many times humor is the best way to introduce decisions of finality. Once, a friend of mine vetoed a deal by saying: "I'm against this deal because there isn't enough direct investor involvement. It's like kissing a pretty girl through a screen door." Humor is a valuable aid because it enables us to discuss even off-limit subjects.

Specific Benefits

Friends not only care for each other—do for each other—but also learn from each other. Often we are able to identify features in friendship which can be mutually advantageous.

I've not talked about platonic friendships between men and women, and yet I am a great supporter of this possibility. I think it's completely demeaning to the ultimate relationship to say that sex must dominate whenever a man and woman relate to one another. They can treat each other with the same high regard and dignity without having to be associated in some business or political venture. Two persons can be complementary without damaging either's integrity.

Persons of Reaction

I use the term "persons of reaction" much like linguists do "language of reaction." I understand these linguists get very excited when they start to dream in the new language they are studying because they know it is becoming very much a part of them. No matter how many languages they know, there seems to be one which they call their "language of reaction." In emergencies they speak it automatically. We have friends who become the people to whom we automatically turn for help—for encouragement—for good memories.

There is nothing scientific about this, but I find that in my dreams my closest friends are doing very natural things. I seldom dream of any one of them doing anything out of character.

Confrontation among Friends

Friends are responsible for each other. Part of that responsibility is the moral obligation to confront—not to punish, nor to embarrass, not even to convince, but to confront with an honest observation. This kind of confrontation has these basic elements:

1. *Timing*—The confrontation should be made at a time when the other person can do something about the matter. Only confront when there is an emotionally healthy atmosphere in which the person can objectively hear the criticism. Never confront as a rebuttal to having been confronted, by saying, "While you're criticizing me, let me tell you something about you." This develops competitive confrontation, which is very unhealthy.

2. *Amount of confrontation*—Only unload on people what they can handle. It may make us feel better to unload the whole load, but our feeling better is not the object in friendly confrontation; it is helping the other person to work on something in the amount that they can handle. We must avoid inundating them or immobilizing them. Criticism has gone too far when it makes people doubt themselves.

3. *Attitude in confrontation*—We should never confront a friend unless we sincerely prefer not to. Never criticize a friend when you enjoy it. This means that we do not argue strenuously for our point once a person understands what we have said. Arguing becomes imposing our criticism.

Normally we are advised to criticize another privately to avoid his embarrassment and to reduce his need to defend himself, but it's also important to do it privately to avoid the temptation to appear superior and a "know-it-all."

Hanging on the wall of the guest room in our son's home is this lovely poem: "A friend is one who knows

you are who you are—understands where you have been—
accepts who you have become, and still gently invites you
to grow."

When Friendship Dies

When friendships die—and they do—life goes on. It
should go on in the best way possible for both. Neither
should stagger through the rest of life crippled as if they
had lost a leg or an arm or half their brain. True friendship
leaves the other an entity. When a friendship dies, I try
to think of these five things:

1. *Admit it, without recrimination.* When we are sure that
a person is dead, we examine the corpse and then bury
it. We grieve for a while, going through various stages,
but we fully expect to come out mature individuals.

2. *Don't let the rejection make enemies.* Just as we are honored to be accepted as friends, we feel deeply hurt to be
rejected. It is a very natural, though a mean trait of our
nature, to let this rejection turn a friend into an enemy.

3. *Keep confidences that you received while friends,* for your
very self-respect depends on it. The natural consequence,
if we divulge confidences, is that we will feel guilty. Also,
from a practical standpoint if we divulge confidences, we
can fear reprisals. The death of the friendship itself hurts
enough without adding to that the hurt of reprisals.

4. *Keep memories.* Good memories are the dividends that
our investment in friendship pays. Don't return the dividends when the friendship dies. We all need to store up
memories for our days of aging, and good memories have
a way of offsetting the grief of the death.

5. *Be willing to establish a different relationship with the person.*
While restoring a friendship that has truly died is impossible, we should be willing to establish another valuable
relationship with the same person; yet, we should not try
to hide from the fact that the first relationship is gone.

It's very fortunate when divorced couples can remain friends even though they know that they are not in love as they were when they married. In the Bible peacemakers are called "blessed." And this is a quality we'd all do well to develop.

The Qualities of Intimate Friendship

When I think of my friends I think of three words: freedom, acceptance, and safety. By *freedom* I mean the quality of being unrestrained—we can be totally open with each other without any apology or without any doubt or rethinking. If we make a mistake, we laugh, not apologize.

When I speak of *acceptance,* I mean the assurance of total acceptance as a person—spiritually, physically, intellectually. This does not mean total acceptance of behavior, because some behavior is undesirable and calls for confrontation. However, friends need to have an acceptance of each other's behavior even when confrontation is necessary.

By *safety* I mean a safe relation that has a secure, buttoned-down feeling about it—a relation with a peaceful harbor where we can comfortably dock alongside each other. We need to feel safe from being used or pushed into a disadvantage; we even need to feel safe in the knowledge that, in a moment of weakness, we'll be restrained from a burst of passion. Safe friends guard each other's welfare. We don't have to fear our confidences being divulged or a remark repeated that exposes our self to hurtful psychological threats. A safe friend doesn't drive us too close to our reasonable edge when others are looking on. Practical jokers are seldom "safe" friends.

Benediction of Friendship

On a night too pleasant to sleep I wrote this to a dear friend of many moons:

During the last few months I have read and reread the thirteenth chapter of 1 Corinthians. I hope I haven't violated these verses by writing them into friendship, but I think you will see the message I see in them: "Friendship is slow to lose patience. It looks for a way of being constructive. It is not possessive. It is neither anxious to impress others nor does it cherish inflated ideas of its own importance. Friendship has good manners and does not pursue selfish advantage at the other's expense. It is not touchy. It does not keep account of slights or gloat over the mistakes of the other. (A friend does not make himself big by making the other small.) On the contrary, it is glad when truth prevails. It knows no limit to its endurance, no end to its trust, no failing of its hope, and in this it can outlast anything. True friendship stands when all else has fallen."

I concluded by saying, "What a treasure you are, my friend. It has been fun riding jumpseat in your success. I know you never expected to swap that truck for a company jet nor leave Hicksville to pick up business interests around the world or become a friend of the mighty, but you have, and I want you to know I am glad. With blessings and gratitude, good night."

A Creed to My Friend

I owe you my loyalty, even to my hurt, but I do not owe you my agreement.

I owe you tolerance and encouragement and recognition of your gift. I owe you part of me—my time—my thought—my possessions and my vulnerability.

I owe you serious consideration of your admonishment of me.

I owe you my forgiveness—a friend who truly forgives does not need to forget.

The Essence of Friendship:

Oh, the comfort, the inexpressible comfort of feeling safe with a person; having neither to weigh the thoughts nor measure words, but to pour them all out, just as they are, chaff and grain together, knowing that a faithful hand will take and sift them, keep what is worth keeping, and then, with the breath of kindness, blow the rest away.

Dinah Maria Mulcokcraig

THINK ABOUT IT . . .

When we understand each other's motives, we can very easily understand each other's actions.

Better a friend with a bad habit than a mean temper.

"I know what things are good: friendship and work and conversation. These I shall have." *Rupert Brooke*

Respect is the only perfect bridge between friends.

8

YOUR FAMILY

The Ultimate Measuring of Relationships

In this chapter, I want to look at the part a family plays in our individual support network. It is not my purpose to decry the reality of family deterioration, even though I could do so with deep conviction. But here I am trying to deal with the reality of the family in our support network.

All about us we see various family patterns: single-parent families, "mingled" families where formerly divorced parents are remarried, and families with the two parents and children fully blood-related living together. All these different "families," no matter which pattern they follow, can be happy (with normal problems, no less) if their "cluster" is healthily magnetized by love.

A family is like a cluster of steel balls held together by a strong unifying magnetism. Each member is separate yet together, drawn by the magnetism in each individual ball and held by the magnetic force of the total. The cluster is flexible, not fixed around a father or a mother. And the mother and father are not subordinate to the children. The cluster adjusts to the changing times, circumstances, personalities, and needs.

In a strong family, love is the positive magnetism that holds it close. On the other hand, hostility pushes us apart, like reverse magnetism in which articles push against each other rather than attract. Such families, when together, resist being close or attached to each other. They have developed an opposite polarization.

I believe the "positive magnetism" concept is superior to the "link," or "chain," concept, because too often we see a large link with all the members of the family hanging on it like keys from a key ring. If the main ring breaks or dies, whether father or mother, the others are left separate and dangling without cohesion. This support system is less healthy.

The family viewed as a chain forces each link to interlock making separate entities impossible. In the magnetized "ball cluster" concept, love's magnetism does not restrict movement, growth, individual responsibility nor our entity. If something happens to one, the others coagulate again in a cluster, simply smaller because one is gone. As the children marry, the cluster expands.

How Many Happy Homes?

Once I asked a prominent psychiatrist what percent of the American marriages are happy ones. He said, "Less than 25 percent." I asked him the test that he applied, and this is what he said: "Both partners would gladly do it over again, knowing what they know now about each other." From his experience with troubled marriages, he felt that most married people think they could have done better and would if they had it to do over.

Routinely we hear in family analysis that the problem is parental lack of time with the family, either by the father or mother, but usually the father. This is not the answer in most cases. This analysis assumes that more time would be profitable and pleasureable. Meaningful time does not depend on the length of time. Such an analysis regarding father failure fails to consider that often when the children are small the father of necessity must spend an inordinate

amount of time in his career to succeed. I have not seen
any evaluation of what it does to a family for a father to
fail. A failing father is not part of a healthy family environment. Part of the demise of the "father" image started
in the Depression when many fathers were unable to provide the financial support their families had come to expect
of them.

Husband and Wife Solidarity

The first step in building a strong family support system
is for the parents to love each other, not only as lovers
but also as friends. When a couple fail to remain friends
they open a large field for competitive games. Some couples, however, seem to thrive on vicious competition. They
set up their in-laws or friends as referees or spectators
and eventually may visit with professional counselors who
frequently do much more refereeing than counseling. But
as competitors they don't want counsel—they want to win
and eventually to do the other in.

Unfortunately, these couples also use their children for
spectators. Eventually the couple perform before anyone—cab drivers, store clerks, fellow church members,
even folks on the street who happen to be standing near
them. The contest becomes the reason for their being together. They would divorce but they have a good competitive game going, and they aren't going to stop it "until
death or neighbors do them part." The home is a ring
with walls instead of ropes. What started out to be an
individual sport becomes a team sport with each trying
to add players. The children are pressured by threats or
rewards to take sides. Friends who try to stay neutral become suspect—peacemakers are as welcome as rain on
parade day.

Soon the reason for the fight is buried in the rancor
and determination to win. Eventually it goes beyond winning to a determination to destroy the "enemy." They

are no longer one; they are not even friends. In the end they have killed a part of each other by killing the best part of themselves, becoming two spiritual vacuums waiting to be indwelled by more evil spirits than before. What could have been a home for love has become its tomb.

In contrast, where the husband and wife are solidly related, enjoying each other without any threats of separation, the family unit grows strong, giving support to all the members.

Ageless wisdom says, "A father can do nothing better for his children than to love their mother."

Parental Authority

I believe in the authority of parents—not just the complete authority of one, though I do believe in the ultimate responsibility of the father. My life in business has convinced me there must be one person with ultimate responsibility. The buck must stop somewhere and, historically as well as scripturally, the best place is with the father.

In order for their authority to be "of a whole cloth," each parent must support the other. When our son was in his late teens he suggested that my failure to consistently support Mary Alice was probably one of the worst things I did. At the plant, working with nonunion employees, I had found that decisions had to be made on "what is right," not on "who is right." That worked well in the plant, but it is not a good principle for home management. My son told me how he and our other two children learned that by giving me "reasons" they could convince me that Mary Alice had made an incorrect decision which I would reverse. I thought I was being morally correct but I was completely wrong. For me to support Mary Alice's decision was the most important thing in order to have solidarity of authority rather than isolated "reasonably correct" decisions. If I were going back through our family life, this is one change I would certainly make.

The solidarity of authority breaks down when parents become competitive with each other for love of the children. We drift into it in such innocent little ways. For example, when a father takes a child out alone he might say, "I know your mother wouldn't like for you to do this, but after all you're only a child once." That is a wedge and a cheap shot for the affection of a child.

One of the most humorous and yet dramatic illustrations of authority solidarity happened when my friend Ron came into the kitchen and found his two young sons hassling his wife to the point of tears. They had her going like a shuttlecock over a badminton net. He walked up behind the two, grabbed them by their necks and bumped their heads together. The blow was just hard enough that they both fell to the floor with big knots rising on their foreheads. While they lay there he said, "Stop hassling my woman. Fortunately for you, we were married before you got here, and fortunately for us, we're going to be married after you leave. Now stop hassling her." Ron looked over and big tears were running down his wife's face. Those two boys had learned a very valuable lesson in the solidarity of parental authority.

Returning to my cluster metaphor, much of the magnetic love starts with the parents and extends to the children. It may be instinctive or divine, yet one quality this love must have is the toughness to provide a consistent healthy authority.

Sigmund Freud said, "I could not point to any need in childhood as strong as that for a father's protection." One of the major functions of authority is to provide protection. Strong authority protects a family by providing clear values, a sense of direction, and rewards for accomplishment.

Too many "authoritarian figures" want to provide punishment rather than discipline. As a perceptive executive once defined for me, "Punishment is what happens when discipline fails." The two should not be used interchangeably at all. Any good organization has to have a strong discipline, and the better the discipline the less the punishment. Punishment should embarrass a parent even though it must be administered.

Almost subconsciously, I think, children feel the need for authority and discipline—even punishment—when they have broken the discipline. One day when our daughter Brenda was in her early teens she told me how much more our neighbor did for his daughter and how much more lenient he was. In fact, it was such a long list that I felt totally inundated and, not able to defend myself, I asked, "What do you make of it?" To which she smilingly replied, "They don't love her—they give in because they don't love her."

No less an authority than Ann Landers corroborates Brenda's story by saying, "Don't be afraid to be boss. Children are constantly testing, attempting to see how much they can get away with, how far you will let them go, and they secretly hope you will not let them go too far."

Part of parental love is concern with the children's education. But it is more concerned with what they learn in the home than what they learn in school. It is easy to abdicate our educational function to the school and then criticize it, as we are hearing so much today. I like what Daniel Webster said: "Educate your children to self-control, to the habit of holding passion and prejudice and evil tendencies subject to an upright and reasoning will, and you will have done much to abolish misery from their future lives and crimes from society." This is real family support.

Maintaining Excitement

Most everyone wants to be married to an exciting spouse, but the problem is that we expect the other to be exciting. The really difficult family problems come when each expects the other to act first in doing the good things.

Mary Alice and I decided, many years ago, that we had to maintain excitement in our relationship. Consequently we are constantly planning some trip, some project, some home improvement, some night out to maintain the fun of being together. On one such occasion it was the day before Valentine's and I decided to be nostalgic and buy Mary Alice a big box of candy. But I also knew she was fighting a diet. Therefore, I went by the hardware store and bought a small chain and lock and wrapped the candy with this, packaged it beautifully and gave it to her as I left town, to be opened the next morning. I called about breakfast time, knowing she would open the package with the children, which she did. And we all laughed, knowing that I had the key and would have a fair shot at the candy when I got back. As I opened my fresh shirt a valentine card fell out of it. We don't do enough of these silly, wonderful things for each other.

Conflicting Compulsions

It is nearly impossible for two to marry and live together without difficulties. I am no marriage counselor, but through the years I have had occasion to observe that some of the most severe problems come from conflicting compulsions. Compulsions seem so reasonable to the person having them. They grow and, because they seem so reasonable, we encourage them to grow. An orderly person, for example, may become compulsive about orderliness, but the compulsion doesn't seem wrong. If some orderliness is good, then complete orderliness is better. First the person practices it and then he or she imposes it.

Almost any good trait can become a compulsion—for example, neatness, punctuality, frugality, and so forth. The trouble arises when the compulsion becomes an irritation or an inconvenience to the other. Mary Alice will pardon me if I tell just this little bit about our experience with conflicting compulsions.

Mary Alice is an excellent housekeeper and, while she would not admit to being immaculate, I would describe her that way. I am more casual, which on occasion some might define as "sloppy." Her neatness and my sloppiness conflict at times. Generally, it's the time when my compulsion for doing all the home maintenance conflicts with her desire to call in some neat professional who needs no supervision.

It works this way: One day I was under the sink cleaning out the drain when I looked over and saw these two lovely female feet and a broom beside me. It always happens, for when I start to work she comes with all the equipment to clean up as I work. There's no way for me to convince her that I will not completely destroy the house and that as soon as I am through then she can have a total opportunity to clean up the mess I have made. She is afraid for me to get that much headstart on her, and so she insists on cleaning as I fix.

Here we have conflicting compulsions. In a saner moment we talked this out and decided there would be no way we could be loving during these periods of conflicting compulsions but at least we could be courteous. We made an agreement not to scream at each other after we found, from repeated experiences, that screaming really didn't solve the problem. There is no solution for the problem; we have to live through it, for she feels completely reasonable in maintaining the neatness, and I feel equally reasonable in doing my own "mechanic-ing." The trick: in periods when you can't be loving, you can at least be courteous. This protects the friendliness of the home.

The president of one of our local insurance companies and his wife heard me talking about "conflicting compulsions" just before leaving for a Hawaiian vacation. Just for fun in the relaxed atmosphere, they listed their own compulsions and called me when they got back home to tell me how much it helped them improve their relationship.

Changing Relations

Compromise is so important in a marriage. When totally dominated, the other becomes "hostilely dependent"—a psychiatric term meaning dependent but angry about it. Part of the changing relationship is in the important area of sex where, as the couple grow older, it moves from urgent to enjoyable; however, it does not move equally with the two partners. When the wife doesn't have a separate income, the husband controls the money and the wife controls the sex. A great many wars are fought on this battlefield. I once asked a marriage counselor what were the major problems among couples, and he said, "Money, sex, and in-laws." However money and sex are so often tied together.

Maintaining a Positive Relation

Part of a positive atmosphere is letting each person define happiness in his or her own way so long as it is moral. We once had a neighbor whose father insisted that the son be happy with the presents he thought the son should enjoy. The son would certainly have selected something else much more important to him. I often thought how the father was defeating what he was trying to do in giving the presents. He was creating disappointment, even hostility, rather than appreciation. It is important to know what the other person defines as pleasure and happiness.

There needs to be some "sitting loose" in the relationship. I would find the lock-step, completely rigid, regulated family a very oppressive environment which would justify Andre Gide's remark, "Families, I hate you! Shut-in living, closed doors, jealous protectors of happiness." We need to be kept afloat by the support of our family, not drowned by it.

We can't lose heart if all our efforts at loving relations in the family are not instantaneously successful. For example, we have a five-year-old grandson, Gregory, who is a combination of philosopher and fighter. Recently his mother went into the church nursery and found him sitting in a corner on the discipline stool because he had gotten into a spitting and hair-pulling contest with another kid. She was taken aback but decided to wait until they were in the car to lecture him. Mary Helen started off real cool. "Gregory, have you ever seen your father and mother spit on each other?" He said, "No, Ma'am." Then she continued, "Gregory, have you ever seen your father and mother pull each other's hair?" He said, "No." There was a long pause in this dramatic questioning that was finally broken by Gregory. "Mom, you ought to try it sometime. It's a lot of fun."

We have a family saying, "Laugh or have high blood pressure." She laughed. Children may be innocent, but they aren't always pure.

Relationships with Our Children

When the children are young, parents must take all the responsibility, but our function as parents is to build into our children a sense of responsibility which will eventually release them from our guidance. As our children once learned from us, there will come a time, it is hoped, when we can learn from them. As we taught them, now they teach us. To accept this joyfully, as evidence of having been a good parent, is one of the rare pleasures of life.

I have not become convinced at all that parents should be "buddies" with their children. A child needs a parent for support. Parents need to realize they are maturing and can't stay young by simply trying to be a buddy to their children. That, to me, is irresponsible. Neither can I agree with Evelyn Waugh, who said, "Perhaps host and guest is the happiest relation for father and son." This is one of the most cynical statements I have ever encountered. It's like saying that when the child is young he is a guest in the father's house, just as when the son gets older the father is the guest in his house. This denies and distorts the real relationship.

When a daughter marries, it's an intimate matter but important. It's a very difficult time for the typical father. No father has ever felt that his daughter married up to her potential. Many of us are amazed how the son-in-law improves by being in our family for a short time and so we're delighted. But few start out meriting our daughter's love. Fathers who are close to daughters have to realize at the time of their marriage they must withdraw for a reasonable period until the relationship between the daughter and her husband becomes firm and fixed. She is now his wife more than her father's daughter and therein lies great pain. She still needs the father's love, but the type of support she needs from him has changed. I cannot speak authoritatively as a mother, but I suspect there is a relation between mother and son which must go through adjustment in order for the son's wife to come into the family support network comfortably and constructively.

The Tyranny of Children

We speak of the children as being the future, and that is true, but they are not the present, for we, the adults, are the present. Therefore, adults for the present, kids for the future. Sometimes I feel that my father lived when a man was dominant and now I live in a period when the children are dominant. Somewhere I missed my day in the sun!

I say that facetiously, for I feel very strongly that the present time for accomplishment is with the adults. It has never made any sense to me for a couple to have children and to spend all their time raising the children who are going to have children and spend all their time raising the children. Somewhere along the way, there is something more to do than raise children.

Foreign visitors to America are forever commenting about the tyranny of the children in the American home.

The children determine what products are bought, what entertainment, what clothes, and much of how the family budget is spent—all based on the standards established by their peer group. And when their expectations are not met they feel "put upon." It's embarrassing to visit a home where the children monopolize the attention and the conversation. It's like visiting a kindergarten in which you have no children or grandchildren. It is not too bad if you don't have to spend too much time there.

Though oversimplified, there is truth in what Sam Levenson, the Jewish comedian, says, "Choose when you want your children to hate you. If they love you when they're young, they'll hate you when they're old; and if they hate you when they're young, they'll love you when you're old." I have seen it happen.

Children seldom misread their parents. I was always surprised how intuitive our children were—how well they read us. For example, one time Mary Alice and I were going off on a trip, leaving the kids at home. Before we left I got the kids together privately and asked that when we came home the house be in good shape because Mary Alice had always been concerned that the house was "probably a mess" while she was gone. When I asked them if they would be sure to have the house clean, they said, "No," not in a disrespectful way, but in an understanding way. Therefore I asked why they had said it. One of them spoke up and said, "It would upset Mother too much. If she came home and the house was clean, she would feel that she wasn't needed." After that, I assumed the kids could do a great deal of thinking for themselves.

The Importance of Family Rituals

Family rituals are important. In all societies families need habitual, special times such as holidays, anniversaries, birthdays when special effort is made to be together.

Even daily rituals, such as reading and prayer together,

promote family strength. For example, when our kids were young we started holding hands during the prayer before meals. It wasn't necessarily because we were so loving, but it gave everyone an even break going for the food. Actually, the hand-holding ritual flushed out any bad feelings around the table—the members who were angry with each other refused to hold hands. Since it was a rule of the house, the offended or the stubborn were permitted to "touch" rather than hold hands. Contact had to be made, though often very slight. On more than one occasion, this generated some of the world's slowest movement as each sibling tried to force the other's hands to come more than halfway. There probably were times we didn't get contact, but the other hands were close enough to feel the sparks.

Then, honestly, there were times we held hands to keep from slugging each other. However, through the years this practice has been one of our better disciplines. Each person knows not to get too angry before mealtime. The choice between missing a meal and holding hands can be a powerful motivation.

Now we are discovering the joy of bringing our grandchildren into the practice. They join hands with us as we pray for them by name. I say "pray for them"—not preach at them. It does give them the opportunity to hear us talk to God about them—how glad we are for their time with us and for our friendship for each other. As we do this, we are building our family support system.

"Talking time" becomes another ritual. Families must take time to talk together. Again, many find the mealtime best, providing TV can be eliminated. Families who find it easy to talk together know that an honest opinion, even a contrary one, deserves respect. They have learned to listen and examine other viewpoints. Family talk isn't parental teachers talking to pupil children, but individuals learning from each other, sharing interesting and exciting observations, thoughts, or questions.

As a child I remember very well having to wait for the second table while the adults ate at the first. I am totally against this, even as an adult, for I have found that many of the good discussions at the dinner table create mutual respect between the adults and children. I think it is important that we permitted our children to eat at the table with our friends because now those friends of ours are also friends of theirs.

Constructive criticism is another vital aspect in the development of the family support function. Naturally we must avoid negative criticism and the laying on of guilt. The Jewish quote is well taken: "Look for the good, not the evil, in the conduct of members of the family." In accepting responsibility for helping each other develop, we strengthen the mutual bond of the family. A child should know by our attitude that our right hand is waiting to hug even when our left hand is punishing.

A Family Philosophy

In recent years my philosophy of family function has shifted from the managerial to the relational. I would have discussed this at the opening of this chapter, but it is new to me, so I felt a little self-righteous preaching a philosophy which I have practiced such a short time. My coming to it is part of the changing relation with our children in which they are now, in many things, my teachers.

When Fred, Jr., was married, he asked that I be his best man since we were best friends. I was deeply honored and sentimental about the situation, so I wanted to return the favor. I offered to tell him the essence of family management. He replied obliquely that he was not going to be an executive but, rather, a professor. He also implied that while I had been successful as president of the corporation, I had not enjoyed the same success in managing the home. Since ours was a close, loving family I was shocked and asked for more explanation. To which he replied, "You never really understood a father's function, for you tried to be president of the home as you were of the corporation. In the company you put production first and relation second. You did the same thing at home. You treated Mother like a vice president and the rest of us as if we were in the line organization. You would pass orders up and down the line, and if we had grievances, which we had first taken up with our supervisor (Mother), then we could bring them to you for final decision." Sensing that he was giving me new information, he smiled and said, "You did the best you could and we love you for it. We operated around you a great deal." I must admit I knew there was a grapevine in the place that I wasn't on, but since I had done my best—even though I had always suspected there was something more I did not know about my function—I didn't feel guilty for it was the best I knew. As we talked he said, "Dad, relation *is* the production in a family. It isn't *what* we accomplished . . . primarily it's that we love each other and secondarily what we do."

For the first time I genuinely understood the essence of family life. Before, I would leave the family after dinner and go into my study, with them gathering around the television. Since I objected to watching television generally, I would cross between them and the set and make a few disparaging remarks about watching television, just to make me feel that I was properly supervising the home. It didn't keep them from watching but it did hurt, at least temporarily, our relationships. Since that time I have tried to think of relations before production, and it has been a very difficult transition. All of my reflexes, habits, concepts, were based on a managerial concept rather than a relational one.

Possibly I can illustrate from a letter I wrote my dear friend Howard Butt, Jr., in the beginning of this period when I was struggling to make relationship primary:

Howard—I'm beginning to see the family in a very different light. The family's primary function is a relationship to create loving relations and secondarily a production unit for developing mature individuals. It is different from the plant, where production is primary and relation is secondary. One hopes, and I believe it is possible, to have both functions running together smoothly, each complementing the other. However, until we understand which is primary and which is secondary, we are not able to make a good, objective decision when one conflicts with the other.

Howard, you can't believe what is happening as I'm writing these words to you. Mary Alice is knocking on the door, wanting to know if I want to go to McDonald's with Brenda, Mary Helen, and our four grandchildren. I believe the Lord is testing me as to my sincerity, for you know that isn't exactly what I want to do right now. Yet, if I'm going to change according to my new knowledge, I must take leave of you and finish the letter when I get back.

* * *

(After 60 minutes or so) Now, Howard, concerning the family. It would be great if I could tell you that now I have learned this new truth I am thrilled, excited, every time I practice it. That's not so. There I sat with my wife, daughters, and grandchildren, doing my best to be relational when I was still thinking about the production I wasn't getting out. However, I did it and I'm glad I did it but I have to be honest that the good feelings haven't quite arrived. I think maybe it is just evidence of our juvenile belief that whenever we do good, we ought to feel good. If doing good made us feel good, then the devil sure would have a poor opportunity; his power would be less than nothing. The fact is, a great deal of the time doing good is unpleasant, but still it's right.

However, honestly I am beginning to have moments

of deep satisfaction putting relationships before production. I know it is the right way to go.

A Tribute

I wish I could have been as good a parent as my children are to our grandchildren.

THINK ABOUT IT . . .

If there were more laughing in marriage, there would be less laughing at it.

Too many marriages start out in bliss and end up in blisters.

It is better religion to be kind at home than to pray in church.

The best adults grow up close to a loving grandmother.

"The starting points of character and destiny in the young begin with home environment and outside associations." *Henry F. Banks*

"If you must hold yourself up to your children as an object lesson, hold yourself up as a warning and not an example." *George Bernard Shaw*

Never teach a child to be a falcon, for one day you may be the prey.

"Give to a pig when it grunts and a child when it cries and you will have a fine pig and a bad child." *Danish proverb*

"It is easier to rule a kingdom than to regulate a family." *Japanese proverb*

When you berate your mother-in-law, you're slandering your children's grandmother.

"Children are natural mimics—they act like their parents in spite of every attempt to teach them good manners." *Anonymous*

So often we expect the worst of our children because we know that they have so much of us in them.

Pray not to get a perfect wife, for she would be a bitter mirror for a fallible husband.

If your wife doesn't treat you as she should, be grateful.

When we cannot be loving, we can at least be gracious.

The Christian paradox is that a man does not necessarily marry the woman he loves, but loves the woman he marries.

III

KEEPING THE LILT
IN LIFE

Through wonderment, urgency, gratitude,
reverence—
life gets its lilt . . . its buoyancy . . . its
enjoyment.

KEEPING THE LILT
IN LIFE

Life needs continual aeration. When it gets heavy, it settles down on us and needs to be lightened up. People should find inspiration and joy in their faith, not just new layers of guilt and condemnation. Jesus said, "I have come that you might have joy." True, Christ came to convict of sin, but the Christian paradox is that in this chaotic, tragic world, we can enjoy a life of adventure and excitement.

Many people live with deep troubles. Someone estimated that about six out of ten of those who sit in church have major hurt in their lives. Therefore, I appreciate those speakers, teachers, pastors and others who lift people's spirits with inspiration and hope. Of course, spiritual aeration must be more than mere humanism. The "blessed hope" is not guilt but grace—we are forgiven, we are free, we have the fellowship of the body and an inheritance immortal. We have talents and gifts. We count. Each of us can make a difference where we are.

If this is not true, then we are fakes. If it is true, then why not exult in it, breathe it in and inflate our sagging souls?

What a challenge to face the depressed with this message

of hope and help. What a responsibility to spread the light and share the lilt. This opportunity gives us something to say, to share.

The Scriptures are full of inspiration and joy. To be inspirational, we don't have to be merely humanistic. Humanism believes in the perfectability of man. I don't. However, I do believe in man's great potential after new birth. We sometimes become so hung up on our lack of perfectability that we overlook our high potential and great possibilities.

The gospel is a balm, a "lubricant." And far too many of us are running without enough oil to keep the friction down and the RPM up!

For me, there are four very important words—*wonderment, urgency, reverence,* and *gratitude*—each of which adds its own brand of aeration to my spirits.

Wonderment

Early one morning I was listening to Carlos Fuentes, the South American novelist. He described the heart of a novel as "amazement." This, I realized, is what I have to be open to constantly. I call it "wonderment," looking openly at those things which cause within me a sense of awe and worship. Someone has said that the true mark of genius is not to create awe in others, but to be awed. Many of us have a tendency to become cynical, closed-minded, disinterested, even bored. Concentrating on our knowledge rather than our ignorance, we lose our sense of awe. In this sense, my ignorance is my friend, not my enemy. It is my playground of the future. I don't need to compare what I know to anyone else. I need to compare what I don't know with the vast amount I can learn. The more we know, the more we realize there's so much more to stimulate wonder.

I experience wonderment when I listen to Philip Morrison speak about the termites of Australia. Some of these small insects are "farmers" that prepare the ground, plant, cultivate, and reap the food for all the other termites. At one time we thought the atom was the smallest unit of the universe, and now we're finding universes within it. Fascinating! When I see writers drawing pictures with words, or handicapped people with incredibly optimistic spirits overcoming their limitations, I am amazed. When I studied the black holes of space, I watched Dr. Hawkins, one of the outstanding authorities on the subject. He's severely handicapped and can rarely get out of his wheelchair; yet he has established himself as an international authority in this demanding area. I'm not awed only by the black holes, but by the spirit of a man like this.

The more you look for wonder, the more you see. It's a discipline. It's easy in life to become jaded and say, "So what?" But that's not the biblical spirit. Paul said in the Scriptures not "So *what?*" but rather "So *that.*" He was all things to all men "so that" he could reach them. He kept his body in submission "so that" he wouldn't be a stumbling block. Paul had a vision and a sense of wonder in what God was doing.

You don't need money to fill your life with wonderment. The poorest person in America can borrow books or look at the wonder of an ant carrying a stick. Sometimes I search the Friday newspapers for all the things I could do on the weekends without money—lectures, concerts, walking trips, museums. Some people are so overcome with what they can't do for lack of money, they're blind to what they can do. Every human being can open his eyes to the wonder in the world.

Wonder has two great enemies: entertainment and acquisition. *Entertainment* satisfies our need to be outside ourselves. The fantasy of TV is often just interesting enough to keep us watching, and just not quite bad enough to make us turn it off. It becomes an anesthetic to our mind. In its dullness we lose the excitement of watching real life.

Acquisition—that other enemy of wonderment—gives us synthetic satisfaction in acquiring things. We use our energy and thought planning and shopping for more things, hoping they will create in us the sense of satisfaction that our previous purchases failed to do.

The other night I walked around our house to look at the paintings on the walls. One I hadn't really looked at for five years. Yet, I could still get excited about saving enough money to buy another painting no better than this one when I hadn't looked at the ones we have. We want to buy books when we have books we've never read. Acquisition is a tremendous enemy of the sense of wonder because our energy and excitement get used up in the process. Acquisition fuels our pride, not our sense of wonder.

Urgency

If you have no sense of urgency, then you have nothing important in your life. Someone has said one of the problems of retirement is you lose your urgency because your priority list becomes level; nothing stands out as having to be done. One of the great motivations of life is that things have to be done at a certain time and in a certain way; you become urgent about them. People who have no urgency can lose their zest. Without important things to do, they feel unimportant.

Yet, we discipline our urgency. Being urgent about everything is actually being panicky, one of the least desirable traits. All my adult life I've tried never to panic. I think one should drill oneself so that in crisis the first reaction is, "Don't panic."

I remember having prepared very intensely for a talk to the Texas Bankers Convention. Sunday night I reached into my briefcase to get my notes for the presentation Monday morning. To my horror, there wasn't a single piece of paper there. I realized I'd left the file in the trunk of my car, which was at a garage being fixed and was totally unavailable.

There I sat, unable to recall the contents of my talk, and the subject was too specific to use old materials. My first words to myself were, "Don't panic." I knew if I did, I couldn't be effective. I spent most of that night recalling, assimilating, and assembling. Thirty minutes before I spoke, I was ready, and the talk was very acceptable. If I had allowed myself to panic, it would have thrown my mind out of gear.

Panic is not part of being urgent. Genuine urgency enables us to focus on the task at hand and enjoy the results of that urgency. I've learned to welcome the positive stress of urgency as one of the greatest engines of an energetic life.

Preparing for a TV show with "Mean Joe" Greene and Craig Morton, I asked Craig, of the Denver Broncos, what it took to be a great professional quarterback. His first qualification was the "ability to relax under fire." Evidently I didn't react as knowingly as Mean Joe thought I should, so he followed up by explaining, "What a pro means by relaxing is to stay in control." He knew Craig wouldn't go to sleep when Mean Joe of the Steelers came at him; he knew Craig had to stay in control or panic. If he panicked, the play was over.

Reverence

The following verse may seem like a strange one for reverence: "How can you say you love God whom you have not seen if you love not your brother whom you have seen?" But this correlation struck me: How can you say you revere the Creator when you don't revere His creation? I hear people talking about reverence for God who have no reverence for man or the world God created. One night Norman Cousins and I were talking, and he told me he had recently returned from visiting Dr. Albert Schweitzer in Lambaréné. As they walked up the hill, a hen and her little chicks walked in front of them. Dr. Schweitzer took off his hat, bowed, and said, "Congratulations, my dear, I didn't know it would be so soon." I admired his spirit of reverence for life!

We can easily say we revere God, yet selfishly use people and even condemn them to hell with a hidden, self-righteous satisfaction—even though God still loves them deeply. We live in a fallen world, but we are still called to have reverence for what God has made. When we look at people as coinhabitors of our Father's world instead of competitors, our perspective changes.

I have to remind myself of this every morning on the freeway. Sometimes I take my own advice seriously enough to make a resolution to do one favor for another motorist on the way to the office. I find that when I pause and let somebody in line without blowing my horn, it affects how I feel when I get to the office. Reverence for my fellow human beings aerates my spirit.

It works toward both man and God. Reverence for the created doesn't seem complete to me unless I reach out and have reverence for the Creator. I noticed on the cover of *Harvard* magazine a statement about DNA being the most important "invention of nature since we rose from the murky waters." I felt rather sad that they couldn't see anything beyond "murky waters." One of the values of being a Christian is that while I can agree DNA is a magnificent, amazing reality, to believe it is God's creation lends so much more dignity and reverence for life.

Gratitude

I've been constantly surprised at how few people feel grateful when I think they should. Many live by the philosophy portrayed in the remark, "What have you done for me lately?" Our son pointed out that most people when they say "Thank you" simply prove they have been well raised, not that they're grateful. I can't demand that others be grateful for what I've done for them, but I can demand of myself that I be grateful for what others have done for me. Gratitude puts a lilt in life.

Gratitude is very pragmatic. For example, Hans Selye, in *The Stress of Life,* points out that according to his research, gratitude is the healthiest of emotions, whereas revenge is the unhealthiest. It's interesting that the Bible tells us to be grateful for all things, and another verse proclaims, " 'Vengeance is mine, I will repay,' saith the Lord." God says not to harbor vengeful feelings, but to be constantly grateful. Here is an example of a modern scientist verifying Scripture.

I used to have trouble understanding the phrase in one of the psalms that God wants our "sacrifice of gratitude." How can you equate thanksgiving or gratitude with sacrifice? But then it dawned on me that when I truly thank someone, I'm sacrificing my ego. I'm saying, "You did something for me I couldn't do for myself." It really is a sacrifice.

Gratitude is the positive interdependence of people, which brings peace; whereas revenge is negative and produces violence. I have nothing I haven't received. I am the recipient of health, education, opportunity—everything. Each morning I need to say, "I am part of this marvelous human race which, though fallen, is so greatly loved by God that Jesus Christ died for it." Talk about gratitude!

Our old nature keeps pushing selfish thoughts and fears into our lives, but if we think of the magnificent work of God on our behalf, and all of His works of wonder, we will be aerated in such a way that we can genuinely glorify our Creator—in wonder, urgency, reverence, and gratitude.

THINK ABOUT IT . . .

A great deal of our excitement, unfortunately, happens to us vicariously through television, sports events, and other entertainment.

The best proof that God is all-powerful is He will win, even though we are on His side.

Praise is the steam that rises from a warm heart.

A great evening of conversation changes a room into a sanctuary.

If you think you can or can't, you are right.

The greatest value of education is to deepen our reverence.

Anxiety is the future; worry is the past.

Many look not in awe but only stare in fear. Relax and look.

ACKNOWLEDGMENTS

My special thanks to

W. Fred Smith, Jr., our son and early collaborator

Margie Keith, secretary—manuscript typist ad infinitum

Rev. Steven Brown, friend and manuscript reader, pastor of Key Biscayne Presbyterian Church

Harold Myra, friend and helpful manuscript organizer, president and publisher of Christianity Today, Inc.

ABOUT THE AUTHOR

Fred Smith—businessman, consultant, lecturer—is president of Fred Smith Associates, a Dallas-based food packaging firm. He was born in Hunting, Tennessee, in 1915. At age twenty-six he became head of Industrial Relations for General Shoe Corporation, responsible for twenty-six plants and over one hundred retail stores. Eight years later, he became vice president of Powell Valve Company. Then after five years, he became vice president of operations for the Gruen Watch Company, a position he held until he opened his own firm in 1955.

Fred Smith currently writes a column for *Leadership* journal, but *You and Your Network* is his first book. He has served on more than twenty boards and trusteeships, including Cummings Incorporated and The Turner Foundation. He holds an honorary doctor of laws degree and was awarded the Lawrence Appley award of the American Management Association. For many years he was active in the leadership of a Laymen's Leadership Institute, chairman of the national board of Youth for Christ, and member of the executive committee of Christianity Today, Inc. He was chairman for Billy Graham's earliest Cincinnati crusade. He has been consultant to such corporations as GENESCO, Mobil, and Caterpillar, and has lectured in over twenty universities and forty-six states and foreign countries.

He and his wife, Mary Alice, have three grown children—Brenda (Mrs. Richard E. Horch), Fred, Jr., and Mary Helen (Mrs. S. S. Noland, Jr.).